LIGHT OF OTHER DAYS

DATE DUE

DEMCO 38-296

Light of Other Days

A Dublin Childhood

Pauline Bracken

MERCIER PRESS

IRISH AMERICAN BOOK COMPANY (IABC)
Boulder, Colorado

To my husband, Niall,
with love

First published in 1992 by Mercier Press
PO Box 5 5 French Church Street Cork
Tel: (021) 275040; Fax: (021) 274969
e.mail: books@mercier.ie
16 Hume Street Dublin 2
Tel: (01) 661 5299; Fax: (01) 661 8583
e.mail: books@marino.ie
Reprinted 1998

Trade enquiries to CMD Distribution
55A Spruce Avenue
Stillorgan Industrial Park
Blackrock County Dublin
Tel: (01) 294 2556; Fax: (01) 294 2564

© Pauline Bracken 1992

ISBN 1 85635 218 8
A CIP record for this title is available
from the British Library

Printed in Ireland by ColourBooks Ltd
Baldoyle Industrial Estate Dublin 13

Published in the US and Canada by
the Irish American Book Company,
6309 Monarch Park Place, Niwot,
Colorado, 80503
Tel: (303) 530-1352, (800) 452-7115
Fax: (303) 530-4488, (800) 401-9705

Contents

1

Blackrock

MY CHILDHOOD was firmly rooted in Blackrock, a small seaside town on the south-east coast of Dublin. It had once been a fashionable watering place, in the time before the railway cut the sea away from the town in 1856. It still had some style of its own and traces of former elegance in the number of large houses in the district where once the nobility had gathered to enjoy the sea breezes. Frascati House, the former home of Lord Edward Fitzgerald and his young wife Pamela, stood among mature trees at the entrance to the town, and Blackrock House, Lisnaskeagh and Maretimo House were large residences at the various entry points to Blackrock. Idrone Terrace at the seafront had 'Idrone Sur Mer' on a parapet halfway down the terrace, looking straight across to Howth. There was a shingly beach, a men's and women's bathing place and a wonderful view right around the semicircle of Dublin Bay. The tides came swirling in, vigorously filling up the bathing places to a good depth for swimming; at low tide you could walk across the sands to Maretimo where the private coves and the harbour of the big house lay, and far out to sea a lighthouse winked irregularly. 'Town kids' would come out in droves in summer and give Blackrock back its original purpose of seaside resort, and small shops such as 'The Lido', 'The Wee Shop' and 'Budinas' met the demand of the visitors for ice-creams and sweets.

Blackrock had several small stores, some of which stayed open as late as eleven o'clock at night. In the main they were run by little old ladies in long black dresses with white hair pulled back into buns, but some were run by family co-operatives and you could be served by anyone from a four-year-old upwards. These shops had names such as 'The Nest' and 'The Nook' and the neighbourhood could not have functioned without them. An abundant supply of milk and bread was their backbone, particularly milk, for which there was no worthy substitute. Headaches were catered for, likewise situations calling for syrup of figs. Wart and toothache cures were stocked and there was always a box of seed for a starving budgie who could not hold out until morning. Boxes of chocolates were built into impossible pyramids on shelves so that rotation of stocks became somewhat doubtful, and a picture of gambolling kittens on the lid of a chocolate box might fade and blur before an actual sale could be effected.

When Easter came around, such shops went in fiendishly for Easter eggs, from the smallest ones to large and plushy types with heavy ribbons and unlikely looking chicks marching across them on glued feet. We loved the artificial chickens which broke out everywhere as the big day came nearer, perched on regular stocks, on boxes of shoelaces and hair-slides and even on the edge of the daily delivery of brightly iced cakes. Such small shops embraced festivals with great vigour as there were plenty of sales to be made in celebration, and the Christmas decorations came down barely in time for the St Patrick's Day and Easter outbursts of merchandise. Rashers were supplied to these shops by a secret source in the country, maybe a brother-in-law of the owner off-loading on an inner ring. They were about a foot long and came wrapped in grease-proof paper and then brown paper and were kept in the ice-cream fridge. They always tasted delicious and most people going to such shops bought a pound or two of rashers with whatever they came to buy. Some shops ran a vague lending library in one corner and customers would thumb through books while waiting to be served. Nurses-and-doctors-type romance was the guide to popular taste.

There were birthday cards, toothbrushes, nibs for plain wooden pens, lighter flints and bundles of sticks soaked in paraffin, the forerunners of fire-lighters. Service was always silent, or with a minimum of conversation for the proprietors had long learnt that a chat with one person would lose them a sale with the next. Only when someone died locally and Mass cards were in demand did they break this rule and indulge in reminiscences while they did a brisk trade in sympathy.

A friend of my father's used to get his cigarettes in one of these shops and one night had a most unnerving experience when he went out at closing time to get some more. As he rounded the corner the lady in the shop was just pulling down the blind and, aghast at the thought of passing the night without cigarettes, he waved vigorously. She waved back and paused, and now frantic at the realisation that the shop was well and truly closed he made smoking gestures at her by raising his closed index and third fingers to his mouth and moving them back and forth. She looked at him steadily for a moment, smiled coquettishly, blew him back a kiss and shot down the blind. As he stood there confounded, the heavy bolt on the back of the door slid firmly back into place. He was even more upset by being taken for a late night cavalier than by the prospect of a night without cigarettes and could never bring himself to go into the shop afterwards.

All groceries were delivered by large shops such as Lipton's and Findlater's and we dealt with Findlater's for the better things in life. As children we enjoyed seeing the change from bank notes whizzing across the ceiling in little brass cylinders from the counter to the money office and back. Some branches had suction tubes to convey the cylinders even more quickly. Two rather vague ladies ran the vegetable counter and they did this at their own pace, putting on and peeling off rubber gloves every time they had to weigh potatoes and calling to one another for the loan of a pencil to tot up the bill,

9

while the customers waited three deep in a cloud of frustration. A large man called Mr Vaughan was the manager of the branch in Blackrock for many years and he used to boom out the orders in a foghorn voice. He brought the whole shop to a standstill one day when he roared out in his northern accent: 'Six dozen of stout for the Mercy Convent'.

Near the post office there was a German pork butcher called Horlacher's and the sausages there rivalled the famous Hafner's sausages of George's Street in Dublin which had the whole of Ireland in thrall. We thought Horlacher's sausages were even nicer and whenever Rowel Friers came to stay for a night after a business meeting with *Dublin Opinion*, his mother always gave instructions not to reappear in Belfast without a few pounds of Hafner's sausages. He invariably forgot to get them. One of us would be dispatched on a bicycle to Blackrock to get some in Horlacher's instead, and he always successfully passed them off as Hafner's on his return.

Wearwool was a small snug wool shop further down the main street. It was run by 'Miss Wearwool', for no one ever knew her real name. Once the little door with a bell on it was closed behind you, the shop was hermetically sealed from the noise outside by the wool-packed walls. Miss Wearwool's woolly cavern was a pleasant place to be, so that we never minded when our mother took a long time to choose a knitting pattern, so cosy and mysteriously quiet was it after the hubbub outside.

Further on again was the Monument Creamery chain of shops. It was cool and clean and smelt like a spotless dairy. Great blocks of golden butter stood on marble slabs and brown-coated assistants spent all day scooping up chunks of it between wooden pats and boxing them into blocks before wrapping them in grease-proof paper. Other assistants calmly built pyramids of butter to a height of their liking and no one seemed to consider these activities as time-wasting. A most popular line in the Monument Creamery was the country butter which had salty water right through it, and this squeezed out between the pats in drops on the marble top. If you closed your eyes while eating this butter you could transport yourself back to the country on holidays, and we were always begging for it to be bought.

There were at least three shoe-menders in Blackrock as this was an important part of the economy and shoes wore down quickly. Every Saturday our shoes were checked for worn soles and heels and the wearers were sent to have them repaired. Repairs took some days and you had to get by for a few days in either your good or your worst shoes until your everyday models were repaired and collected. Bradmola Mills in Carysfort Avenue made nylon stockings, a relatively new product which appeared just after the Second World War. They followed the fine-mesh cotton stockings which were exported to the States where they were called 'Balbriggans', Balbriggan being the name of the town in Ireland in which they were manufactured.

McKinley's hardware and drapery store had a delightful arrangement whereby customers, without paying even a deposit, could take home items of their choice 'on appro' as it was known. My mother frequently took home cardigans, shoes or even a summer dress and tried them on in the comfort of her own home before deciding for or against purchase. This could take some days and no one was in any hurry about it. If she decided to keep something, she put it carefully into her wardrobe and left it there for sufficient time to be able to take it out and wear it without the guilt of buying something out of the housekeeping money. The bill was paid at the end of every month and all in all it was a comfortable method of shopping.

There was a small newspaper shop called 'Variety' in Carysfort Avenue and the man who ran it lived in the back with his mother. When you went in there was always a wait and you peeped through a glass door with a lace curtain behind it to see whether one or the other proprietor would rise from the couch in front of the fire and come out and serve you. 'Mr Variety' had a system whereby he sold comics at fourpence each on a Saturday morning when they came in new. He also bought back second-hand comics from the previous week at a penny each, and the boys used to come in and slap their old comic down on top of the pile of second-hand ones, and take it up again with three others, to make the price of the new comic. 'Mr Variety' never noticed the method of transaction and must have suffered a slight loss in turnover without realising it.

A wonderful smell of fresh bread used to come from O'Leary's Bakery and Café which stood at the fork in the main street at the top of the town. Outside the bakery stood the heavy stone cross which marked the boundary of 'The Pale', the area of British jurisdiction stretching southwards from Dublin Castle.

There was a shop in George's Avenue which we called 'Ma Flanagan's' and this was a strange little place, half sitting-room with large sagging couch and fireplace, and half shop, with no dividing line between the two. Miss Flanagan mounted in the window arrangements of the roughest apple tarts imaginable, side by side with small pyramids of potatoes on lace doilies. She also sold lemonade and an assortment of sweets and bars of chocolate. We used to go in for fun to see what Miss Flanagan was wearing, for her wardrobe was as varied and imaginative as her window dressing. One day she had a large thin mat wrapped around her waist and held in place by a piece of cord, as she bustled about the shop tidying things up because, as she said, the health man was coming. The civic guards often went into Miss Flanagan's in the evenings for lemonade and apple tart and to catch up on the news, as it was happily believed she was a reliable source of information from the underworld of Blackrock.

We were proud Blackrock had many famous people either associated with it or living in it. Seán O'Sullivan the painter lived in Avoca Cottage on our road and we visited his home frequently. He once took me out into the garden and turned my head this way and that, presumably because he wanted a child for one of his paintings. He then returned me when my sister asked timidly, 'May we have our Pauline back, please, Mr O'Sullivan?' Brian O'Nolan, alias Myles na gCopaleen, alias Flann O'Brien, lived at number three Avoca Terrace and I remember seeing him at midnight Mass in the school chapel.

The Misses Findlater of Alex Findlater and Company, the wine merchants, lived in 'Glensavage', a large house beyond Avoca Terrace, and the German ambassador, Dr Katzenberger, lived further up Avoca Avenue. Eamonn de Valera lived in 'Chesterfield' on Cross Avenue and as small children we misunderstood the notice 'Trespassers Will be Prosecuted' and thought it meant 'electrocuted' and that the electric chair was housed in the security man's box at the gate. At the point where Cross Avenue intersects Booterstown Avenue, Kevin O'Higgins, Minister for Justice and External Affairs, had been cruelly assassinated in 1927 on his way to Mass in Booterstown church.

Maurice Walsh the writer lived in 'Ard na Glaise', an old house shrouded in trees at Stillorgan Park; and Thomasheen James, Maurice Walsh's man of all work, the same Thomasheen James as in his book *Thomasheen James – A Man of No Work*, used to walk down our avenue every morning. His trousers were tied with string under the knee and he kept his eyes so straight ahead that we used to ask him the time every morning and would always get the same answer: 'Ten after nine'. Count John McCormick lived at 'Glena' at the foot of Booterstown Avenue and James Joyce lived for a time in 'Leoville' on Carysfort Avenue.

2

Home

OUR FIRST HOME was on Mount Merrion Avenue, a leafy boulevard one mile long, celebrated because John Boyd Dunlop, the veterinary surgeon who invented the pneumatic tyre, had once lived on it. I remember our home mainly as the house to which my mother brought back a new baby and the place where I dropped a little lead sheep down behind the bath while I was entertaining myself by washing it, and lost it forever. If you stood at the gate at the front of the house you could see the sea through the gates of Blackrock Park, and the bay was always full of sails. A river ran through the lane at the bottom of the long garden behind the house and once, to our open-mouthed amazement, children had emerged from the river-bed having entered it at further up and come down under the road. A door in our garden wall led to this high adventure point which was strictly out of bounds to us.

When I was about five or so, we decided to move house. I was very frightened as I thought the house itself would have to be moved and I was afraid it might fall on some of us in the process. To my relief, it proved otherwise and with some sadness on my part as I had never lived anywhere else, we moved ourselves instead to a larger house in the district. My deepest regret was the infinite loss of my little lead sheep and I pondered deeply whether I could come back and ask the new people if it would be possible to look for a sheep under their bath. Although I rehearsed my speech many times for the stranger who would open the door, I was too small to go back alone and no one wanted to accompany me to lift me up to the bell, so that I was one sheep down for the rest of my life.

'Rosemount', the new house, was to be our home until we grew up. Once settled in, it never occurred to us that we could move again, live anywhere else or that anything about the house could be changed. It was our home, large and splendid in some respects and possibly quite odd in others, but home it was and that was it. If little mushrooms grew on the back of the scullery door, and they did, they were scraped off and forgotten about until they grew again – plans were not necessarily drafted in for a new door. It was a big house with three storeys in front and two at the back and five staircases. Standing well back from the road it had a long sunken lawn in front and we loved its detached loftiness. The grounds of Carysfort Convent lay spread out between us and the Dublin Mountains, and the only sign of industrialisation was the occasional streamer of smoke when a small train puffed its way across the base of the mountain, servicing Carrickmines and Foxrock from its starting point at Bray, and running out of sight to Dundrum, Ranelagh and Dartry until it reached its Harcourt Street terminal beside St Stephen's Green in Dublin City.

We were a family of six, plus parents, plus indoor help, and so people were continually going out and coming in through the hall door. The latchkey was left in the lock by day and often spent a full night sitting outside. A cavalier attitude prevailed towards security and anyway it simply would not have been worth any thief's while trying to move about our house unnoticed. High wide granite steps led up to the front door and a thick copper-beech hedge was trained up each side which lent the house a pleasant and elegant air. It was nice to sit on the steps and look across the convent fields to the Dublin Mountains in summer.

As the house was very spread out the only way to locate anyone was to stand in the hall and shout loudly. Doors would then open on different landings and contact could be established. In one corner of the hall stood a hat and coat stand which had so many items on it that it looked like a group of old men standing in a circle having a chat. The hall table was piled high with correspondence and its drawers held prayer books, keys, screwdrivers, clothes brushes and various fuses, all of which were only sorted out about once a year, generally at Christmas time. One year I found my own letter to Santa Claus in the drawer and presumed he had dropped it going through the hall.

Three clocks kept the family punctual. A grandfather clock stood in the hall and bonged out each hour; Westminster chimes called up from the dining-room as each quarter was reached, and from the drawing-room mantelpiece came the piercing ping ping of the ormolu clock, a sound which penetrated the air sweetly. As a result we all developed a clear sense of time and its fleeting passage.

THE FAVOURITE ROOM was the study. It was the clearing-house for all operations and my mother loved it and inhabited it. Heads came around the door frequently to say 'I'm off now, Mum', or 'I'm back now, Mum', in the form of emotional card-punching that goes on in large families. The study had two very large windows facing south and south-west respectively so that once the sun was in the sky the room caught and retained all its heat. Both windows had wide wooden seats and while the one facing south was usually occupied by my mother, the other one was piled high with current and out-of-date telephone directories, copies of *The National Geographic Magazine* and old copies of *Time* magazine. There was nearly always a fire burning in the grate except during very fine summer spells, and the settee and low leather armchairs were constantly occupied. Central heating had arrived in domestic Ireland but was not considered a priority in our home, and an alternative form of heating to open fires was supplied in the form of a red enamelled electric fire which shone brightly at the corners of its coils, as if giving warning that it might withdraw its contribution at any time. A large bookcase furnished the back of the room with more books covering the top of it. It was so splendidly full that it was practically impossible to extract a book.

A cabinet gramophone with a playing arm like a crowbar happily ploughed up the 'seventy-eight' records of our choice and the needle in its playing head had to be changed frequently. It was difficult to extract a needle from the small tin box in which they were kept, without dropping them all into the hearth rug each time. When the Black Box record player came on the market, other people got one but we were content for some time to come to play the new extended-play records through the wireless on a pick-up.

The heavy velvet curtains in the study made it a cosy place to be at any time and we would run down and dry our hair at the fire there after a bath and hair-wash, rather than use a hair-drier. One evening my sister was sitting by the fire in pyjamas thus occupied when the hall door opened and voices were heard in the hall; it was friends of my parents whom they had met out on a walk and brought back for a cup of tea. She saw the study door handle turn and leapt for cover behind the curtains, crouching on the window seat and deciding what would be her next move. The root of the problem was that she had no dressing-gown on and so she sat there as tea was brought in and the conversation warmed up while she started to freeze. She eventually reached such a low body temperature and high panic level that she sprang in one leap from the window seat and dashed through the door, violently rocking the budgie's cage and disappearing with a whirl and a bang. The visitors rose up screaming and tea and cake flew all over the place so that it was some time before peace could be restored. Our home was not a place for people of a nervous disposition.

Whenever the study was getting too lived-in, a tidying spate was introduced over and above the weekly maintenance. One of my brothers had the knack of 'putting a look on it' and within a short time he would restore the room to its correct level of polished hearth, blazing fire, gleaming furniture,

17

magazines arranged suitably and a general air of control.

The budgie sang in his cage for eleven years and contributed to the conviviality of the study; in spite of the continual opening and closing door, it was the place to be most of the time. An ongoing battle for survival went on between the budgie and the cat, whereby the cat would slide in unnoticed and hide behind a chair until it eventually gave in to temptation and climbed up inside the curtain to have a go at the cage. The cage would begin to swing and the budgie flutter, the cat would be ejected and life would flow on as usual. The budgie throve on haphazard care and affection resulting from the general pressure of events. He learned to talk nearly as well as the members of the household and only got fresh water, clean sand and new seed when life allowed. He survived all these vicissitudes probably because this breezy attitude brought him nearer the conditions of the free and the wild. Being a cheery bird, he sang, chatted and gave wolf-whistles all day long with a shut-down of the service at the same time every evening when his cage cover was dropped over him. My mother loved him dearly and he would talk away as she rustled the newspaper she was reading in the window seat under his cage or talked on the telephone.

He was smart enough to lower his voice at appropriate times and would murmur gently on a warm summer's day or go through his wisecracks for her as she relaxed with a book or some knitting. One day, after a few songs, he fell backwards off his perch and died, his tiny claws crossed piously. My mother cried all that day and said that he 'looked lovely in death'.

Saturdays were particularly nice in the study. After lunch we would all crowd in around the fire and exchange the news of the week, with my mother acting as chairperson for the panel and my father dozing gently for the first time in his busy week, *The Irish Times* held firmly in his hand. Someone would try and edge it gently out of his grasp but he always woke up and refused to relinquish it, claiming that he had not been asleep at all.

NOWADAYS, the basement of our house would be termed 'garden-level' but it was a basement all right. The kitchen doubled for a social centre for our friends on account of the privacy it afforded. No one else had such an amenity as a large warm private gathering place and friends gravitated to it, particularly on cold evenings. We sent away the Beeston Boiler when we came to the house and installed a large-scale Aga cooker instead, the Model E, of which we were inordinately proud. It gave the kitchen such a 'once and for all' look, and permanence was the thread which ran through our lives.

The arrangements of the kitchen were very suitable for many activities. It was a brightly-lit place with a large scrubbed table in the centre and several smaller ones scattered about, with bentwood chairs all around the walls and a flagged floor. The Aga kept it permanently warm and one of my brothers used to go down there at night to practise dancing like Fred Astaire. He had been brought to the film where Fred jumps from table to table and chair to chair without missing a beat, so he would set up the radio and practise privately, leaping from the Aga to the furniture around the kitchen with a view to doing so professionally when he grew up.

Suppers were brewed up nightly and people passing through the kitchen usually checked the Aga oven doors in case anything interesting was cooking silently within. A cupboard in the kitchen was known as 'the press beside the fire', although there was no visible fire in the area. It served as a medicine cupboard and had rows of bottles of pills in it, their labels long blurred. Bottles of Mercurochrome abounded, some lying on their side having long since oozed their rich red liquid into the brown paper lining of the shelves; alongside these were bottles of gentian violet which made psychedelic patterns on the paper where they stood. Apart from these stocks there were always new bottles of the same preparations waiting for use, boxes of Elastoplast and tins of Zambuk, Union Jack Paste for warts, Antiphlogistin for poultices and TCP for gargling. Nobody ever questioned why there should be about three lots of everything on the go at the same time.

The lower shelves held bottles of Jeyes Fluid so large that

at one time a plague must have been anticipated. Maybe some previous owners of 'Rosemount' were responsible for some of the stocks in this cupboard, for no one school of medicine buying could have accumulated such a hoard. The cupboard even offered horse medicines and we didn't ride. Somehow we never got around to throwing things out as the war was in recent memory and had made hoarders of our parents. One never knew when something might come in useful.

The cupboard bulged to such an extent that you had to put your back to it to close it. Once closed it could only be opened by inserting the blade of a knife in the centre slit. People opened it cautiously to prevent an avalanche, anointed themselves suitably and then closed it again. The medicines stayed gently warm from the proximity of the cooker and whether or not their efficiency was impaired by the heat was debatable. It was years before we bought a smart and hopelessly small medicine cabinet for the top bathroom, transferred the up-to-date contents of the 'press beside the fire' to it and threw out the remainder of the preparations.

The pantry beside the kitchen served its purpose admirably by keeping food cool to freezing point. A whistling draught came under the adjacent yard door and completed a circuit in the pantry before whirling out again. There were five wide shelves at the back wall which were curiously curved in the centre because of dampness, and the items on them huddled together by sheer force. These could include large jugs of milk, cut glass bowls of jelly in the setting, covered bowls of soup in the making and other spillables. The accident ratio was negligible as everyone took great care and nobody ever complained about the arrangements or took a stand for straight instead of curved shelves. The floor was of the coldest stone in the world and used to sweat blearily from time to time. We may have had a well under it, as there were many in the district as marked on the Ordnance Survey map. No one was ever mildly curious about renovations and life carried on efficiently in the prevailing circumstances.

THE YARD outside the pantry was occasionally a place of drama. It was constructed on a level about two feet lower than that of the neighbouring property, and in torrential rain all the excess water from their extensive garden drained into our yard, flooding it and blocking our shores. So it was that, on stormy nights, visitors to the kitchen might come on a strange sight: four inches or so of water gently lapping the Aga and, as kittens were a recurring phenomenon in our house, a box of them sailing around on the high tide.

The cry would go up and we would be wrenched from the warm security of the study fire to join forces in the great swill-out operation. Instructions and brushes would be handed out by one of my brothers and we would be posted at various points to brush out the flood. Special lamps were kept for such emergencies. These were actually candles stuck down into jam jars with string handles, since torches and bicycle lamps could not be relied upon to be in working order at all times. By these lights and the lights of the pantry all the leaves choking up the shores would be pulled out and everything would be under control once more in a surprisingly short time. The kittens, still sleeping, would be transferred to a new cardboard box and put on a low shelf in the hot press to recover from any chills sustained, and life would revert to normal as if nothing had happened. As this came about three or four times a year during the storms at the change of the seasons and we were nearly always caught unawares, it just settled into our life as something which had to be lived with and was rated as being of no particular consequence.

The side door to the house was in this yard and the means of opening and closing it were somewhat unusual. A chain ran on the inside of the door from the snap-lock to a hole at the centre door, out through the hole and ended in a rubber cone. To open the door you merely pulled the cone. At night the 'snip' was put on the lock and security was assured for the wee hours. A friend of one of my brothers called one evening and tried the side door first. When he eventually went around to the hall door, he said, 'I flushed three times and got no answer'.

21

THE HOUSE WAS well furnished with washing facilities, with a special bathroom in the basement for the maid. The main bathroom at the top of the house was a large ornamental box of a room, gracefully built out over the granite steps and supported by Corinthian pillars. It had a long casement window with the flimsiest of catches and although it opened quite easily, no one ever took the final step out through it to land in a heap below.

The sources of water were two, a normal-sized boiler in the hot press and a copper geyser in the top bathroom which gave out a reasonably efficient flow of piercingly hot water, but which cooled when it hit the large bath on lions' feet below. It was a serious offence in our house to 'take someone else's water' and baths were booked carefully. The contenders were many and reservations were announced somewhat threateningly, in case a lesser soul might partake of the source without conscience. The geyser was run on gas and had to be lit very carefully, letting the water run first, otherwise it blew up with a large bang. If I saw a hot water tap running in somewhere like Bewley's I lunged at it in panic and turned it off immediately, so deeply ingrained was the dictum that hot water must not be wasted. We used a soapless powder called 'Amani' for our weekly hair shampoo. It came in sachets and looked like custard powder and we had to mix it in a cup of hot water and pour it over the hair, lumps and all, as it was not quite soluble.

OF THE THREE smallest rooms in the house the one facing our nice neighbours was often occupied by a brother with a good singing voice. He would go in, settle himself comfortably, forget about life and its many demands and run through his repertoire. Time and self suspended, sonorous verses of 'The Road to the Isles' and 'Annie Laurie' would float out the window as he availed himself of the excellent acoustics, and our neighbours once asked us whether we had a music room on that side of the house, so regularly were they treated to recitals.

It was not an ordinary house in that it had a picture

gallery each side of the top landing and this constituted an attractive feature and a useful one, for my father, who was a prolific watercolourist, hung his paintings there; otherwise they were in danger of taking over the house between exhibitions. As I was deeply into adventure books at the time I thought it highly likely that there might be a secret passage up there, as such were usually situated along galleries in stories of haunting. When there was no one around and things had settled down generally on a dark evening, I would go up and spend time carefully removing pictures one by one, and feeling the wall space behind them for promising papered-over doors, expecting a 'click under pressure' and a 'groaning swing back of a metal door'. If Angela Brazil's heroines could descend by a secret staircase encased in a wall, maybe with some determination I could do so too. I also went over the floors of the galleries carefully in case a knot of wood offered promise of similar adventure.

OUR BEDROOMS had very high ceilings and had originally been heated by gas fires. When we came to the house as small children there had been some great gassing scare in Dublin, so our parents had all these fires taken out in case of accidents. The result of this caution was that the rooms were extremely hard to heat and the one I shared with my sister, which faced north-east was an upstairs tomb. When we woke on winter mornings we were often able to scratch our names with a fingernail on the light covering of ice that coated the inside of the window. We had a Valor oil heater which sobbed out gasps of warm oily air and nearly asphyxiated us, much as the gas fires were expected to have done, and we would take our eiderdowns off our beds and wrap ourselves in them when we were up in our room doing our school homework. The problem then was that once we were so cocooned, with only head and one arm exposed for turning pages, we would nod off within the fat folds, which necessitated 'opening back' periods in order to get through the homework load without falling asleep.

THE DRAWING-ROOM was a pretty, over-furnished room, full of brocade chairs, comfortable and dainty and quite a warm place, as it was situated over the kitchen where the Aga cooker burned cheerily night and day. It should have been a family room, except that we had to keep it as the major reception room and it was therefore less frequented. A large painting of a monk praying gave the room an air of tranquillity and it was the room where all the violin and piano practice was carried out down the years. The long window with wide window-seat looked out on the lawn and front drive, so that trainee musicians could monitor the comings and goings as they played.

Every Christmas a huge Christmas tree was set up in one corner so that movement around the room was severely curtailed and anyone getting too warm by the fire was in danger of pulling back their chair and backing straight into the tree. This tended to happen regularly during the Christmas festivities and we came to regard the depletion of the Christmas tree ornaments as part of the occupational hazards of celebrating Christmas. It was in this room that Dr T.J. Kiernan, then Minister Plenipotentiary to the Holy See, fainted from boredom. He had found himself in the corner of the chesterfield with a boring person at some party in our house and, because of the limited movement in the room due to over-furnishing, had been unable to escape. Being a polite man he had endured his situation until he finally keeled over in a faint and had to be revived. Downstairs, gulping a glass of whiskey to bring back even a reduced feeling of well-being, he had confided in my father as to the nature of the faint and they had laughed uproariously together over it.

ON A LOWER LANDING we had a playroom or 'nursery' as it was grandly called, and it was still referred to by that name long after all the toys had been put away for good. Beside it was the dining-room, a draught-free, soundproof room where my father usually worked at night on *Dublin Opinion*. When it was well heated with an open fire it constituted a nice working place but, in the strange manner of the house, if it were not heated it proved an ice-pocket, so much so that the food nearly fell from lifeless fingers in the winter when the temperature dropped suddenly. A mahogany clock with Westminster chimes and a lustre jug furnished the mantelpiece and we liked to examine the lustre jug by firelight to admire its range of colours. A short flight of stone steps led down to the kitchen and the current maid clattered up and down them, bringing up courses at meal times. When we girls graduated to wearing backless slippers the sound of our feet was like pistol shots on the steps, but no one ever thought of having the steps professionally covered to minimise the noise. Such factors were just absorbed into the general life of the household without comment.

WE HAD A SMALL abundant garden at the back of the house with seven or eight good apple trees, a plum, pear and cherry tree respectively and splendid raspberry canes which yielded fruit a hundredfold. The garden was so crammed that it was a wonder there was enough nourishment in it to sustain it all. There was a vague vegetable patch to one side where the occasional lettuce sprouted and where I had once buried two poached eggs which had got out of hand on me in the pot and which I did not wish to have discovered in the waste bin.

Our gardener was a man greatly reduced by hardship who lived in a cellar in town and we called him 'Mac'. He never had much to say but he enjoyed keeping up with the general life of the household and would often make surprise comments after long periods of silence. He was having his lunch at the kitchen table one day when one of us came in and dumped down some schoolbooks. Mac leaned over, picked up a copy of Virgil's *Aeneid*, perused it and put it back with the comment, 'Very dry'. One year he threw himself into an orgy of pruning of the fruit trees and ripped off branches with great flair and without having discussed the operation in advance. My father took a serious view of the depleted trees and had a private talk with Mac, whom we did not see for some time afterwards. The following year the fruit on the trees was so heavy that we had to prop up the branches but Mac, being a thorough gentleman, never alluded to his success as a pruner.

The large garage to the side of the house had a broad shelf with a treasure trove of items on it left by the previous owners. These included a full crystal radio set which we never got working, great tablets of wax whose purpose we never divined and an ear trumpet which was very useful for playing grannies. We had a second freestanding garage, which my father converted into a painting studio at one stage. It wasn't insulated or heated and before long the paintings began to wrinkle in their frames, so he gave it up as a studio and it was converted into a bicycle shed instead.

In summer the lawn was the clearing place for friends. Being long and sunken it was the perfect shape for races, and solemn-faced children would arrive for 'training'. Parachute jumps with umbrellas off the top of a ladder were in vogue for a while as were imaginary horse races, with the jockeys dressed in pyjamas and wellingtons, beating their own hindquarters as they went around corners. There was a huge sycamore tree at one end which lent a gentle shade on sunny days and we sometimes had tea on the lawn under its patronage.

3

Dublin Opinion/
Radio Éireann

EVERYONE THOUGHT that my father was marvellous. He
was a very tall man with a ringing step and he wore a black
town coat and an Anthony Eden hat going to work each day.
As he held himself well and wore spectacles, children sometimes thought he was Mr de Valera and it amused him to say
that, yes, he was, when they asked him. He was a man of
many parts, an artist, writer and top-ranking civil servant,
with many other interests, as well as being a 'family man'. The
term 'family man' really meant having a family, as it was not
usual for fathers to spend much time in the company of their
children at the time.

My father's initials were 'CEK' for Charles Edward Kelly,
and they were famous initials as they were in the corner of
every cartoon he drew for *Dublin Opinion*. *Dublin Opinion*, Ireland's national humorous journal for forty-seven years, was
highly popular long before I was born. My father had founded
it with two friends, Tom Collins and Arthur Booth, when he
was only nineteen years of age and it was not surprising that

we grew up thinking it was the best magazine in the world. It came out monthly and our domestic life was built around it.

Dublin Opinion followed the fortunes of the politicians in cartoon, aphorism, prose and verse. It also carried satirical articles and it never failed, in forty-seven years, to meet its publication date. It had first emerged in 1922 during the Civil War when nobody had much to laugh about, and the pessimists said that it could not last. It did. People became conditioned to enjoy it so that sometimes it was hilariously funny, and other times more apposite than funny, but it was truly loved and devoured each month when it came out. Contributors included Maskee, Till, JOD, Rowel Friers, W.H. Conn, W. St John Glen, Seán Coughlan and Temple Lane. A host of other contributors came and went and often contributions were found unopened after a period when the pressure of offers became too great for Tom Collins, my father's co-editor.

The magazine was put together each month in the large sunny offices in Middle Abbey Street, opposite the Irish Independent building, and my father dropped in every day at lunchtime from his job in the civil service to bring in the work he had done the night before in the form of fine pen and ink cartoons and drawings. The workload was heavy but there was always a welcome for us children in the office and tea and biscuits were generally on the go. An uncle of ours also worked in the office but didn't take a lot out of himself as he used to switch on the light with a walking stick, lest he err on the side of labour intensive performance. Rita Gubbins completed the quartet and she quietly ran just about everything and everybody. She managed to pull in a sizable amount of advertising every month and she organised a circulation list for overseas, which served emigrants and missionaries all over the world. Often the advertising was so great that it had to be held over to the following month and this happened particularly at Christmas.

My father would come home every evening by train, march over the iron bridge at Blackrock Station in the fresh east-coast wind and stride up George's Avenue, a direct wind tunnel from the Dublin Mountains. He would tune into the active scene for an hour or two, enjoy his meal and then settle down to work on *Dublin Opinion*, producing satirical paragraphs and amusing articles as well as cartoons. For the three weeks of the month which led up to press deadline there was much for him to do. Once the paper had gone to Cahill's, the printers, he would let the whole pressure slide off him and wait for the arrival on the bookstalls of the new edition. After a week or so the engines would start revving gently again. He had lived with this rhythm since he was at the end of his teens and it had become second nature to him.

When it was coming towards press date he would take out his big drawing-board each evening and set it up on his mahogany desk, pick through his fine collection of pens, India ink, white inks for touching up jobs, razor blades for scratching out errors, hard and soft pencils of the full range, all neatly distributed between the two drawers of his desk. If he discovered that some vital item had been tampered with or even appropriated by a daring homeworker there would be hue and cry, so this did not happen often. He would then plunge into work in a room apart. With vast bursts of creativity he would produce cartoons in pen and ink, working from a small black notebook in which he had been jotting down comic ideas every day. Most of the notions or themes were political and were often the crystallisation of his lunch-time editorial meetings with Tom Collins. Their criterion for the inclusion of a cartoon or aphorism was that it had to make them laugh first, otherwise they did not expect it would make anybody else laugh. The ideas tumbled out so fast that my father would often do several cartoons in one single sitting, and then he would get lonely toward the end of the evening's output and gravitate, board in hand, to finish off a drawing beside the study fire.

When the cartoons were finished he would show them triumphantly to my mother for her approval. The cover was always the largest and most important drawing. She would make good positive suggestions, was always quick to notice the inadvertent dropping of a government minister from a snowballing or swimming scene and she was his best judge.

One of us would then make a plate of sandwiches and bring it up to him as his supper beside the fire, for he was always ravenous after a night of creative output. Sometimes he would feel gregarious and unwilling to shut himself away for an evening's drawing. He would elect instead to draw in the study and would tuck himself in by the fire in an armchair, drawing-board tilted on his knee with a dangerous arrangement of ink bottles set up nearby. When the drawing was getting difficult he would request silence from the sitting tenants with a loud 'shhhhh', raising his blood pressure and lowering his popularity at one time, as he endangered the prevailing atmosphere of gossip and warmth. Very occasionally the dreaded possibility would become a reality and a bottle of black ink would slide off the chair to land with a crash in the hearth. Everyone would jump up, someone would run for a wet cloth and heads would be bumped in the great mop-up. The steady black flow across the hearth would be staunched, the drawing would be inspected with heavy breathing for any minute specks and the bottles would be set up in a new adjacent site. An odd time the razor blade would get lost and the sides of the armchairs would be searched fearfully with fierce warnings about the cutting off of tops of fingers. It would be found, relocated on the mantelpiece and an atmosphere of animated calm would be restored.

Often a drawing was so intricate that it took several successive nights to complete. The full-colour Christmas edition, the bumper summer edition and the election numbers would all get special treatment. The current drawing would be left set up in a separate room for a few evenings and it was then that I would slip in unnoticed, select a pen from the range and add another twig to a tree, a supplementary lump of snow to a winter scene or another hair to a politician's crown. I would then wait to see my work in print and would craftily enquire about the circulation level so that I could gauge how many households and individual readers would be feasting their eyes on my work, acting out my dreams of one day appearing in print under my own name.

Dublin Opinion played a great part in forming public

opinion in Ireland. The captions under the cartoons became household bywords and the phrases coined in it went into the English language of the country. Some cartoons became national favourites such as 'Céilidhe in the Kildare Street Club', depicting traditional Irish set-dancing in a club which had been the exclusive stronghold of the British and pro-British before the country changed hands, or 'The Night the Treaty was Signed', demonstrating the rush for jobs along the Cork to Dublin road when skeletons lifted their grave slabs and joined in the quick flurry for opportunity. Billy Glenn's 'Ballyscunnion' scraperboard drawings were much prized and the originals often asked for, as were the dreamy evocative scenes of Dublin long ago, done by W.H. Conn. Lord Brookborough of Northern Ireland asked for the original of a cartoon showing him going out for the evening with a comely lass depicting the Republic, while someone minded their baby of 'co-operation'.

The two editors, my father and Tom Collins, developed an uncanny sense of timing down through the years and they occasionally scored a bullseye, such as the time they had the launch of a space craft on the cover of *Dublin Opinion* on the same day that the Russians successfully launched their first sputnik. When a major campaign and referendum were launched on the abolition of proportional representation in the voting system in favour of the straight vote, my father drew a cartoon which clearly explained the campaign. He showed a schoolroom with a master and three boys. The master had drawn three apples on the board and was explaining proportional representation to the lads: 'Under PR each boy gets an apple; under the Straight Vote the big boy gets the lot'.

The clergy absolutely loved the magazine for its lack of vulgarity or meanness, its downright funniness and the way it kept an eagle eye on the goings-on in Leinster House. The ever-expanding circulation included just about every mission station abroad and priests, nuns and brothers waited eagerly each month for their up-date on matters at home through the medium of its pages. As children we were very impressed that 'our' magazine went as far as China where the Maynooth

Mission was particularly active, and the foreign stamps which came into the office found their way into our stamp albums.

Brendan Behan who was a popular figure in the 1950s liked *Dublin Opinion* very much. He used to call across the street to my father, 'How's it going, Charlie? I liked last month's!' I was going down Grafton Street with my father once when this happened. Brendan roared over such a greeting that I did not know whether to be delighted or embarrassed, when everyone stared as my father waved to him.

AS MY FATHER WAS Director of Radio Éireann for many years and Director of Broadcasting for a time, we were treated to much radio listening at home. When he came in each evening he would switch on the wireless as he naturally had to monitor programmes. 'Question Time' with Joe Linnane, 'Poetry' with Austin Clarke, 'Round the Fire', a programme of traditional music and storytelling with host Din Joe, 'Drawing and Painting' with Marion King, 'Making and Mending' with Peadar O'Connor and 'Listen and Learn' with Aindrias Ó Muimhneacháin all combined to form a background of supplementary sound in our home. There was also the tantalising tinkle of money in a tin cup for the winner of 'Information Please', and symphony concerts were performed as we exchanged gossip in undertones. Micheál Ó Hehir's voice and sport were one and the same thing, and it was said that it was possible to follow a match from one open window to the next while passing through any country village. When we went to Seapoint or Dún Laoghaire in the car in summer and parked at the seafront, the same voice could be heard from open car windows. The sponsored programmes were part and parcel of living. We ate our midday meal to the céilí bands of the Mitchelstown Creameries programme and 'The Kennedys of Castleross' were hot news each week. We would skim home on bicycles along Sydney Avenue to hear each episode. 'The Foley Family' was another long-running programme, but I secretly disliked it as the family in the story always seemed to be at each other's throats.

One great spin-off of such proximity to the national broadcasting service was my father's habit of inviting people home for a meal. Visiting orchestral conductors and soloists would come out and have an evening away from the strain of rehearsals and performance, and my mother liked to entertain them *en famille*. It was the time when the Radio Éireann Symphony Orchestra was being built up and when broken postwar Europe had many good musicians looking for contracts abroad and several of them found their way to Ireland. They knew nobody and were often marooned in hotels, so they always accepted immediately when invited home for a meal and a bit of fun. On these occasions we were the commis waiters and at one time it seemed to me that I had lit the cigars of one half of the musical personages of Europe and served creamed potatoes to the other half.

In the course of those years the symphony orchestra came under the baton of Hans Schmidt-Isserstedt, Francesco Mander, Edmond Appia, Sixten Eckerberg, Mosco Carner, Jean Fournet, Jean Martinon, Carlo Zecchi and Milan Horvat and they all came out to visit us. As these evenings progressed the musicians would sometimes jump up and grab their musical instruments, which they always brought under cover, and then there would be folk music from the heart of their wartorn countries. They often joined up into impromptu trios and quartets and literally played the night away. Francesco Mander once fell ill with near-pneumonia while he was staying in Dublin, and the staff in the Standard Hotel in Harcourt Street were so good to him, nursing him back to performance level, that he didn't need to cancel any engagements. Naturally he would never stay anywhere else when he came to Dublin. Sydney McEwan, the Scottish tenor, who was a priest, became a close friend and loved to come out and join in whatever was going on, such as mediocre cricket on the front lawn. In the evening he would sip a glass or two and then run through some of his repertoire of Scottish songs with Rose Ó Brolcháin at the piano.

Another favourite visitor was Dr Denis Hurley, Archbishop of Durban, who would telephone each time he came to

Dublin, arrange an evening out and dismiss his driver on arrival so that he could relax totally in surroundings foreign to the episcopal scene. He would dissolve into unhierarchical giggles at anything that amused him and he liked to eat a large dinner and to ask his commis waiters for recommendations. He would make exquisitely funny remarks, quaffing his glass or so of wine and exploring family life. He greatly enjoyed after-dinner chorusing and would join in lustily when the pianist had the party up and going. One year among the fellow guests we had Delia Murphy and her husband, Dr T.J. Kiernan who had been Minister Plenipotentiary to the Holy See and they sang until the ceiling was lifted. This was all my father's doing, as he always invited a good pianist or two along on the evenings the archbishop visited us. One night during a boisterous rendering of some old favourite, a glass of wine flew off the top of the piano and landed in the lap of the archbishop. He thought it was the funniest thing ever and refused to be wiped down until the song was over.

These visits went on for several years and I was already making plans to storm Durban and be the toast of the Archbishop's palace when a fatal mistake was made. My father invited a friend who was a lovely light pianist, but alas the man was also a great sodality man. He plied our cherished guest with questions about the state of the Church in South Africa and the role of the laity there. What was irresistible to the sodality man was totally resistible to the archbishop, and having listened politely for some time, one eyebrow raised and a smile on his handsome face, he said, 'I fear we have a Tertiary in our midst'. No one could retrieve the situation as our pianist friend murdered the archbishop's jolly evening – 'Our' archbishop never came back for any such evenings. Somehow our beloved guest never lifted the phone and invited himself out as he had done for years, and we sorrowed about it, sadder and wiser about the ways of archbishops and how they liked to have a few precious hours of free time.

Among the many people my father met in the course of his work was Sir Hugh Roberton, founder and conductor of the world-famous Glasgow Orpheus Choir. Whenever the choir came to Dublin, a recording of their performance was made and broadcast by Radio Éireann, and Sir Hugh would make all the arrangements through my father. Hugh Roberton was a kindly man; I remember him because I liked to sit on his knee when he came out home. In 1951 the choir was disbanded as Sir Hugh was retiring and the singers did not want to go on without him. It was decided to give the last performance in Dublin rather than in Glasgow, as Dublin was only visited occasionally and the emotional level would be containable at the close of the performance. Accordingly the concert was arranged for the Capitol Theatre and we all went off to hear it and sat in the box reserved for my father for all concerts. We knew all the Scottish songs and rejoiced in them. It was a lovely occasion, with the choir singing as one human being, and when the last song had died away and the last encore had been given, Hugh Roberton bowed first to the audience and then to his beloved choir. Immediately tears began to run down the faces of the singers and one by one they came down to him, shook his hand and went off stage. We were sitting on our row of bentwood chairs witnessing the whole spectacle and I can remember the impact of the collective adult emotion which followed the bitter-sweet concert. Hugh Roberton then took his last bow on the platform to a standing ovation and the curtain came down forever on the Glasgow Orpheus Choir.

AS DIRECTOR OF BROADCASTING, my father often had tricky situations to handle. He actually enjoyed these and could tackle people with splendid aplomb. One such situation was the arrival of Father Peyton in Ireland, the 'Rosary Priest'. He had come to spread his mission and naturally he went first to Radio Éireann for discussions as to how the broadcasting service could be utilised in his work. My father reviewed the situation carefully as he was both a good executive and a deeply spiritual man. In fact it was my father who implemented Josephine Hurley's suggestion that the feast of the day should be announced each morning on the opening of the station. He also loved the rosary and said it with us every night, but what he did not want, and decided should not happen, was that the rosary should be either turned off or talked against in most of the households in Ireland were it to be broadcast in full as Father Peyton wanted. The arguments went back and forth and the Archbishop's office in Drumcondra let matters take their course. Eventually my father's thinking won and Father Peyton departed a bewildered man when his request did not meet with agreement. My father later heard unofficially from Drumcondra that the right decision had been made.

There were also delicate situations to be met in-house in Radio Éireann. On one occasion when the Minister for Posts and Telegraphs was invited on a tour of the studios he was ushered into a new sound-studio only to find an attractive male scriptwriter deeply involved in kissing one of the female announcers, without too much resistance on her part. The Minister bowed gently and withdrew with a wry comment that studios could be versatile areas, which was not always a bad thing. On the same trip it was discovered that there were no biscuits to go with the cup of tea to be offered to the Minister before he left the premises. In fact there was no budget at all for the Director of Broadcasting and my father took half a crown out of his pocket and slipped it to someone to go out and get a packet of ginger snaps.

My father created a milestone as regards the employment of foreign musicians in the Symphony Orchestra. He wanted them because he knew it would bring up the standard of our own players who had not been exposed to the international music circuit, due to travel restrictions during and after the war. He met with much opposition in this but it all melted away one afternoon when fog prevented a world-famous cello soloist from flying in for rehearsals for a concert of great importance. The guest conductor had already arrived and it was a serious situation. A French orchestral player, Maurice Meulien, who played first cellist, leaned over to his music case and took out the soloist's part and offered to play it. He did so to perfection to the delight of the conductor and also the orchestra. When Maurice Meulien was asked how he could give such

36

a superb performance at short notice he replied that it had been in his repertoire from the time he had been a student. After that, foreign musicians were welcomed by the orchestra.

The Hospitals' Request programme once gave rise to a national crisis. There were many long-term patients in sanatoria around the country, well enough to follow programmes regularly and, to an extent, to become emotionally involved with a presenter of their liking. When the presenter, Kathleen Dolan, made arrangements to get married, the marriage bar operated, which meant that she would have to leave Radio Éireann. Kathleen's 'goodbye announcement' came over the airwaves rather like the abdication speech of Edward VIII and patients nationwide were devastated. Radio Éireann was stormed with letters and calls from people saying patients had become seriously ill as a result of Kathleen's impending departure, and the station was under siege. It was deemed wiser by my father not to allow the emotional bond to become so strong ever again. So a roster of two women and one man was organised and the situation was brought under control. This decision was to have an effect long past its usefulness, and well after my father's time, of barring presenters from using their name in the title of their programme and it was a long hard battle for 'The Gay Byrne Show' and other shows bearing the presenter's name to grace the programme schedules.

MY FATHER WAS ALWAYS alive to visible beauty and went around painting watercolours in his mind. When he took us out for drives he would suddenly say, 'Just look at that ... how's that for a view?' and sometimes we did not know what we were supposed to admire and ended up gasping in admiration just to be in on things. Great bursts of praise for nature would issue from the driving seat and someone in the family once said that while other people admired views, we ate them. One Hallowe'en my father was so disappointed with himself for breaking off an attractive leafy twig from an apple, just as he was admiring it, that he got some black thread, bound back the twig in place and had us all admire it. Then he ate the apple appreciatively himself. Kees Van Hoek the Dutch journalist who wrote for *The Irish Times* for many years once mentioned that he had met my father on the top of a bus approaching Merrion Square. He recounted that he had been made descend from the bus by my father, to admire the many varieties of flowering trees that grew side by side along its north side. It was, of course, my father pointing out the beauty around him, although I'm sure that he did not really take Kees off the bus for the purpose.

When my father got off the train at Blackrock every evening he would check the seascape and sometimes he would transfer his impressions of it to paper in the form of a splendid water colour, when he found a few spare hours. How he managed to fit so much into his life was a mystery to everyone. Membership of the Dublin Sketching Club and the Water Colour Society, with paintings presented for exhibition to both groups every year and subsequent sales at the shows, when the red dots seemed to go up on his work first, were activities which he took in his stride. He was continually sharing his talents with others and would sometimes take promising painters out in the car on a Sunday morning, to show how to catch a scene in water colour.

He was always opening up other people's horizons and people loved him for it. We were served art like porridge, something naturally good for us, to be taken regularly. Paintings by Frank McKelvey, Maurice McGonagle, James A. O'Connor and other Irish artists were on the walls at home, as well as his own, and each year some of us were brought to the opening day of the Royal Hibernian Academy and often to varnishing day as well. As small children we amused ourselves sometimes by getting down the bound volumes of the 'Pictures of the Royal Academy of London', dating from 1892 onwards, to look through them. On holidays we visited Paul Henry at his home near Carrigoona on the side of the Sugar Loaf mountain and I remember being small enough to view at floor level the pictures he had stacked on the floor of his studio. My father was also a member of the PEN Club and would regale us with the eccentricities of its members. Lennox Robinson, who was on the committee for many years, once said of a non-contributory committee member, 'He reminds me of a half-cooked sausage. You cannot eat it and it is too good to throw out'.

My father was always introducing us to different worlds and we occasionally paid a visit to Maynooth College where a friend of his, Dr J.J. McGarry was a professor. The premises teemed with clerical students and it was the draughtiest place in the world. Huge stone corridors had open doors at either end and the wind howled around corners, so the priests and students must have needed to dress heavily to survive. Dr McGarry would think up interesting places to visit: the museum, the church and even the great kitchens where we saw lay brothers forking huge hams out of steaming pots and carving them up for dinner. I wanted to impress the learned man and so I turned to him once and said, 'Ah, xylography, I see'.

He looked at me with knitted brows and asked, 'And what is xylography, if I may ask?'

'The art of carving,' I replied. I had found the word in the dictionary when we were looking up words for the game 'The Minister's Cat', and it must be one of the few times a Maynooth professor was inadvertently challenged by a midget who came off best.

4

Mammy

WHEN SHE was not reading or actively engaged in running the household, or out somewhere with my father, or on some private excursion of her own, my mother loved a nap. She would slip into bed for an hour or so in the afternoon, to be awakened by the maid with a cup of tea. Then she would get up in the best of form, freshen up and get on with her day. We looked forward to being sufficiently grown up to be able to take a siesta too, as we thought it was a great arrangement.

My mother was of the view that no doors are closed to you in life except the ones you close yourself and so we were encouraged to explore gently whatever life had to offer if it was basically wholesome. She was a good student of human nature and was not hard on people as she understood the changing nature of existence; she liked to take life as it came and was not beyond giving surprise answers to strangers. One evening as she was leaving the church by the side porch, having slipped in to say a prayer, she had to pass under heavy scaffolding, since church porches were always being either widened or narrowed. A man ran out to warn her that the area was dangerous. 'But I live dangerously', was her enigmatic reply as she disappeared under the scaffolding and out into the evening, her shopping basket on her arm, and none of the trappings of a commando in evidence.

She was not a person for joining committees, but now and then, in a fit of goodwill, she would become involved in fund-raising or sales of work. One year she went in for making mayonnaise for the Carmelite building fund and was very pleased at the amount of money she raised for them at their sale. A week later reports began to come in of mayonnaise blowing up in kitchens all over Blackrock but she was not unduly worried. She assured us that the main thing was that the building fund had benefited by her industry.

She was small and blonde and very pretty and she loved going out formally, thinking nothing of transforming herself from the role of busy mother into a soignée creature in a matter of half-an-hour, sweeping up her hair and donning just the right dress. One evening, thinking that her dress was a little low-cut, she took up a little Irish lace dressing-table mat and positioned it perfectly where it was needed, before going off to stun them all. Her solutions were often instant and nearly always successful. Whenever she wrote anything practical like a shopping list or a school excuse, she never hesitated at all. So direct was her approach that we thought that she could write a school excuse with the handle of a brush. The only drawback from our point of view about instant lists was that you could find yourself in Blackrock with a shopping list of items, so swiftly written that it read on the lines of 'lomabaes', 'large wheam', 'faking bounder' and you were expected to bring back tomatoes, a large cream and baking powder. It was hard to know what to do, whether to risk coming back without the mystery items, bring back something by guesswork or phone up to be told to be sensible.

My mother's bunch of keys wove a dominant thread through our early life. They were attached to a small key-ring, spraying out in all directions so that they almost formed a sphere, and some of them related to pieces of furniture long past recall. Although of an unmanageable shape they kept getting lost and, with crisis mounting, we would all hunt for

41

them. With nerves at breaking point and someone's future about to be ruined, they would at length be retrieved from some mildly astonishing place. They went missing once when we had an important guest to dinner and the drinks cabinet in the sideboard was locked. The guest was due and the apéritifs were going to be non-existent so we were all called down to recite a decade of the rosary for the recovery of the keys. At the close of the decade someone shifted their position and nearly broke their kneecap on a spherical metal conglomeration on the floor. The keys were graciously restored and greatly to be praised were the ways of the Lord.

My mother sometimes did things which startled my father. She once got out of bed at about one o'clock in the morning, put on the light and rustled in the wardrobe for a while. She then drew out a hat and tried it on and stood there smiling at herself in the mirror in her nightdress and hat, adjusting her headgear this way and that. There was always a logical explanation for her actions. She had gone to sleep worrying about what hat she would wear to a forthcoming wedding, and woken up with the solution. A hat she had overlooked would do perfectly well for her outfit if it were trimmed appropriately, and so my father lay there blinking at her mildly as she got back into bed with a satisfied expression and a short explanation. Another time she put a clothes-peg on the cat's tail 'to see what it would do'. The cat ran squawking around the kitchen like a figure in a cartoon, unable to get it off and quite hysterical. My mother laughed so much she couldn't get the peg off its tail and had to go for help to retrieve the situation.

When we were very young she gave us the very occasional treat of a screaming competition. On the maid's day off we would go down to the kitchen, close all the doors and take positions around the table. The rules of the competition were strict and contestants were only allowed one scream per heat, otherwise they were disqualified. Each bloodcurdling yell had to be different in style from the preceding one and a really good scream was received with applause. The winner received a bar of chocolate, or some such prize and the judge's decision was final. This was my mother's way of keeping the upper hand, whatever the situation.

She loved to tell a story against herself and related how once when she and my father were coming home by train from Wicklow, she had hugged up to him when they were crossing the footbridge and said, 'What a glorious moon! We should be sleeping in Wicklow tonight'. To her shock, a strange man had looked down at her and disentangled himself and then she saw my father's form vigorously bobbing along a few people in front of her.

Occasionally she would take a nap in a bedroom other than her own, and she upset someone very badly by doing this on one occasion. One of my brothers was going through the first stages of dating and depended greatly on sartorial help for his conquests. One afternoon he was dressing for some event where girls were to be present and as he finished his toilette he took up position in front of the mirror, picked up an imaginary piece of fluff from his lapel and surveyed his blazered image. Then he burst into a verse of Marty Robbins' 'A White Sportscoat' and had just finished a short dance routine to his own reflection in the mirror, ending with right arm outstretched, when my mother stirred in a bed across the room. He was absolutely furious and she promised never to invade his room again.

My mother loved poetry and was always dipping into volumes of Longfellow, Browning and others and she was familiar with every poem in *The Oxford Book of English Verse*. We got to like it too and would read out sad poems to each other to see could we burst into tears, which we sometimes did. William Allingham's 'The Fairies' was a sure-fire, particularly the verse about little Brigid who died of sorrow because her friends were all gone after a period of seven years away with the fairies, a very long period of time to our minds.

Whenever my mother visited a friend's family with children in a similar age group she used to go through short periods of dissatisfaction with us. These miracle workers would have made all the Christmas cakes at a young age, received prizes for maths and Irish and older ones would have played hockey for their province. We would be regarded as duffers for a day or two and there was no way we could handle this withdrawal of approval. We were poor at maths, indifferent at Irish and undistinguished on the hockey field. Moreover, we had never been allowed to make a Christmas cake in our lives. The turning point would come when we would be all dressed up and setting off somewhere and she would suddenly smile at us delightedly and restore us to favour.

We really loved her and were always trying to siphon her off for ourselves. This never worked, as once she had agreed to go for a walk or do something different with one of us she would take pity on anyone else around and reverse the whole situation. We used to moan at her that if she could, she would have brought the budgie along on a string for the walk.

AT THAT TIME, women served as interpreters to their husbands about the doings of the family. Men and women allegedly reared their families together and presumably fathers all loved their children, but in the majority of cases the fathers were remote people and did not communicate directly with their offspring once these had started to grow out of young childhood. Husbands were filled in regularly by their spouses on the progress, or lack of it in the family, but did not come into direct contact and it therefore came as a surprise when fathers were sometimes put in the role of disciplinarian. The poor men were not really to blame for their lack of public relations, as the system of the time did not encourage it. In some families the men were even thrust into the role of tyrant, particularly about such matters as meals. As there was indoor help in many homes, meals were quite rigidly adhered to and this kept the household strictly on tracks. It also meant that the help also knew exactly where she stood as regards her time off. Men tended to arrive home at the same time every day without fail, as train travel was popular, and they were as conditioned to receive their meals as Pavlov's charges, so variation in meal times was rare. I remember being out for a walk with my mother and some of the others and having to run helter-skelter all the way back in order to lay the table and start the evening meal in the absence of indoor help. I am sure

44

my father would happily have read the paper and waited for half an hour or so, but he was so conditioned to punctuality that he would have been very taken aback to find the home deserted and no overt preparations for his return.

Fathers automatically got the outside of the roast, the meatiest part of the corned beef, the major share of the kidney in a steak and kidney pie and just about everything good that was going. My mother was no different from everyone else's in her lavish treatment of him at mealtimes and any deviation from this pattern would have amounted to a degree of betrayal. I had a friend whose father had been taking hot milk in his tea as long as anyone could remember. This involved using a saucepan to heat it at the last minute and serving the milk in a little jug with a lid on it and a saucer under it. It was a great nuisance as it had to be prepared for every cup of tea he drank and he always had one after meals. One day a member of the family decided that she just could not go on heating milk, putting it in the little jug and presenting it, so she made up her mind to ask her father whether or not he would get along without his hot milk. This was a real show of courage, the biggest confrontation before Gary Cooper faced the man who hated him in *High Noon*. What would happen? Would the roof blow off? The family waited in locked silence and the intrepid family member returned triumphant. After twenty years or so of hot milk in his tea he had looked up pleasantly from his paper and said, 'Whatever you like, I don't mind', and gone back to his reading.

I WAS A CHILD WITH a thirst for life which far outstripped my capacity to keep up with it all. Coming halfway down a family of six I more or less reared myself, and as I operated on many fronts besides the family front I often reported late or inadequately to headquarters. As the hours of the day were insufficient for my purposes I slid in and out of the family structure avoiding collision where possible, and went about my business with an air of independence which belied a fragile make-up. I had a great dislike of the investigations and sortings-out which continually go on in large families and I

45

avoided them where possible, so that I was regarded as a secretive child. As I never had much to conceal I really earned this reputation through my lack of co-ordination of my activities. I regarded the world as an exciting place, to be explored at any price and I vowed to myself that I would not rest until I had seen it all, once I realised that Ireland was not its centre. Any time I was brought to nearby Dún Laoghaire and saw the mail boat pulling out for Holyhead, I experienced real pain that I was not on it, sailing to adventure.

My mother called me 'Doubting Thomas' as I was a logical child and usually saw the flaws in adult explanations and activities. I was at a children's party once at which a magician was performing and one of his tricks was to put a stick of chalk into a box with slates, ask a child its name and hey presto, find that the chalk had written the name on the slates all by itself. He rattled the box and then stunned us all by producing this result. Then I noticed that the clever chalk inside the box had not been written with and asked him, quite innocently, how that came about. The poor man got a nasty fright and bit the head off me to the surprise of everyone at the party.

The family arrangements suited me reasonably well and I would have been very content with life except for one great shadow. I could never tell anyone what was on my mind, if it did not make attractive listening. I continually lost items of apparel as I slipped from one scene of activity to the next and I could never bring myself to report the losses. I could not understand how others could announce airily that they had lost something, and so I had recourse to Saint Anthony instead, promising him my meagre pocket money and paying up dutifully every time something was recovered. He worked hard on my behalf but he really could not keep up with the stream of petitions, and the losses usually drew ahead of the finds.

When I was about eight, I lost my dancing pumps but they were the only ones I was likely to have and I didn't make the loss known. I was simply unable to announce breezily that they had vanished and take the investigation or scolding on stream, and so for lack of pumps I was put out of the dancing class. The situation dragged on and I lost weight steadily, hanging around the school while the others were learning lovely dancing. Snow came and I can remember flying down the slopes at Stepaside on a toboggan, sadly thinking that all this would be great if only I could find my dancing pumps. Finally my hair began to fall out and my mother got seriously worried about my failing condition. Questioning proved unsuccessful and eventually I was brought to Doctor Shanley in Merrion Square for diagnosis. After careful probing the doctor ascertained that I was in a decline over this item of occasional footwear and the whole situation was brought under control by the purchase of fat, black, shiny, new pumps and a return to the dancing class.

MY TWIN BROTHER THOUGHT that having a girl twin was the most unfortunate thing that could ever happen to a boy. When he went to school he sternly advised my mother that it must never be known, as he thought that he would be in for frightful teasing. Another brother thought there was some sort of cachet about being twins and asked my mother to call him and his brother 'the twins' and exclude me from the arrangement. Once when my brother encountered a double-yolked egg at table he turned pale and refused to eat it, but my mother only laughed and told him that that was what he once had been and not to be so touchy about it. Things were always halved between twins and I remember constantly receiving half an orange or half an apple. I looked forward to the day when I would have a whole something for myself.

Like most families we had our own special tortures. One was to heat a teaspoon in a very hot cup of tea at the table and apply it to the back of your unsuspecting neighbour's hand. This always obtained a dramatic response but the perpetrator ran the risk of being asked to leave the table, when the matter was sorted out. Another torture, also carried out at the table, was 'paralesiums'. This was a ball-fisted thump on your neighbour's thigh and it produced such a funny pain that the recipient did not know whether to laugh or cry.

The 'night hand torture' was in vogue for a good while. We would wait until someone was just about dropping off to sleep and then slide in alongside their bed in the dark at floor level. The torturer would silently raise a hand about three inches from the face of the dozer, who, sensing something awry could open an eye and jump up yelling. It was important to leave the door open a little and a distant light on to get the full effect. When we became used to this torture it was abandoned and forgotten.

I realised when I was quite young that my mother greatly disliked the job of drowning kittens. As Winnie the cat obliged us with a family about three times a year, this sad task came around regularly, and so I took over the job at an early age and depleted the little families down to two each time. I used to put everyone out of the yard and retire there until the assignment was finished, and this arrangement allowed Winnie and ourselves to live in relative peace.

ONE BROTHER had a passion for practical jokes and these kept him intensely busy. Apart from the usual ones he learned from comics he spent time thinking up complicated ones which he built into his repertoire. For some time he had been observing the working pattern of men on a building site a certain distance from the back of our house. At five-to-one each day the foreman would blow a whistle for the lunch break and the men would throw down their shovels and clump up to the Nissen hut to boil their kettles. My brother set about collecting whistles until he found one with the same pitch as that of the foreman. He waited at his open bedroom window each day coming up to one o'clock and blew the whistle early. The men would throw down their implements and come up to a blast of language from the foreman who would send them down again. When the foreman changed his whistle, our joker changed his, and this trick was kept up for some time without the originator losing interest.

All giddiness at the table was forbidden and as I sat at the end of the table with a brother on each side I was in line for their sallies of uneven quality and for blame for laughing at

48

them. Giggling was always my downfall no matter how hard I tried to suppress it, and as my parents were totally firm about misbehaviour at meals, I often had to pay the penalty which was to 'take your dinner and go down to the yard to eat it'. Plate in hand, half-laughing and half-crying, I would sway out of the dining-room and stand on the landing outside, moaning with silent laughter and trying without much hope to regain my composure. I would put my meal on the landing table and knock and plead for re-admittance. The apology would start well and then, as likely as not, I would be overcome once again and the whole process would have to be repeated. The others never seemed to get caught and I was regarded as the ringleader of all giddiness, from the first shudder of silent laughter.

Giddiness and a readiness to laugh were characteristics of children at that time, as we had no television to watch and were thrown on our own sources of entertainment. We lived life rather than watched it and on a much less organised basis.

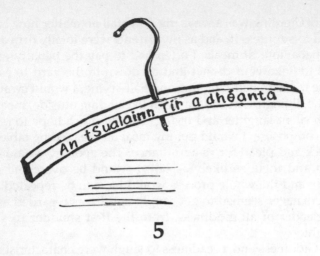

5

Education

I HAD A BEST FRIEND who shared most of my waking time. She was thin with flying reddish-brown plaits, and between us there was enough energy to generate a power station; we considered life an action-packed adventure and saw ourselves obliged to fit everything possible into the normal time span. We passed the early milestones of life in tandem and had several secrets to keep, particularly the 'Secret of the Silver Strand', which we could not possibly have shared with any other human being.

We had been on a picnic to the Silver Strand in Wicklow with my friend's family and had gone off together to reconnoitre the area. A ramble down the strand was decided upon and we were wandering along, heads locked in conversation, when two men came out from behind the rocks heading for a quick dip in the sea. They were as surprised to see us as we were them, as they were clad in the altogether, and they stood stock still for a moment before dashing for cover. We gazed at one another in shock and disbelief, being still very young and growing up in a time of censored publications, and then we got so overcome with laughter that we had to fling ourselves

50

into the sea to recover from the impact. We laughed ourselves inside out and eventually had to let the current carry us down shore to join the other members of the picnic outing. On arrival we could only rock backwards and forwards in spasms of laughter, naturally enough without any explanation. Food was withheld to no avail and we laughed right through the meal, wiping our eyes on towels. We travelled back in silence after an afternoon in disgrace and I was put out of their car at the end of my road, still shaking with suppressed laughter, my friend heaving silently in the corner of the back seat. For ages afterwards we had only to meet each other's eyes and mouth the words 'Silver Strand' to bring about paroxysms.

Sexual matters were not mentioned at school, apart from some mystifying references. We were told to be careful about 'nakedness', but this seemed highly irrelevant to our lives apart from washing, and we were advised not to 'disport' ourselves, which word I had to look up in the dictionary, having failed to get an explanation of it in class. The dictionary advised me that it meant 'to frolic, gambol, enjoy one's self, show animation'. I found it very puzzling indeed.

Curiosity about the facts of life eventually began to gather as we were at the stage of amazing revelations on the part of friends. One classmate advised us that the seed of a baby was located in the roof of a man's mouth and that it was extremely dangerous to kiss a man for longer than three seconds, unless you were married to him, as this was the way in which babies were started. We decided to be very careful indeed when this activity came within our orbit.

Around this time I was paying regular visits to the dentist to have a bridge put on my teeth and I discovered women's magazines with all their offers of help and advice. I saw an advertisement in one of them for a booklet entitled *The Glass Woman – Facts of Life Explained* and I was enormously interested. It was promised under plain cover and when I confided to my friend that we were about to crack the nut of reproduction, she advised me to have the book sent to another friend's address for confidentiality, since both the friend's parents worked outside the home and it would be easier to extract it from the post. In due course the book arrived and a special afternoon was planned after school hours to study the contents. With a cosy fire in the grate and some tea and apple tart for support, we opened and read the first few pages. The atmosphere was encouraging but we couldn't understand half the words as they were in Latin, a situation eased by the fact that the book was carefully and copiously illustrated. When we came to explanations about men we choked on the apple tart and couldn't bring ourselves to read it between splutters. Order restored, we took a decision that it might be a sin to read that section until later on, but that it would be perfectly all right to read the section about women and how they functioned internally. It was thrilling stuff and we looked forward to an exciting future. Having absorbed as much of it as we could, I took home the book to read it when my conscience permitted me to do so, something I hoped would happen soon. A few days later my mother found it and took it away to read. She told me some time later that she had found it very enlightening, having borne six children without a word in print on the subject.

MY FRIEND lived at five minutes' distance by bicycle and this facilitated our constantly being together. Whenever we were apart we corresponded compulsively and when she went down with jaundice I immediately wrote to her to keep her appraised of life. She answered describing her jaundice in detail and adding that she was delighted that I was 'game to take the risk'. A week later our entire family went down with jaundice, then a highly infectious illness. When we recovered we decided to check on infectious diseases before entering into correspondence, and then we devised a scheme whereby we could correspond without being put to the expense of a stamp. We cut the stamp and used the postmark from an envelope and glued this combination carefully to an unused envelope of exactly the same colour. Pale blue Basildon Bond was the note-paper which was all the rage at the time so this was easily enough matched. Next, her name and my address were written on the envelope, and on a similarly treated envelope my name and her address were written. We then crossed out the respective addresses and wrote 'Try at ...', giving the correct address. Writing to each other like this was done simultaneously to heighten the excitement of seeing whether or not the letters would arrive. They did and the system began to work perfectly for us, with letters passing back and forth, and Blackrock post office quite out of the matter. After some time my father, as a high-ranking official in the Department of Posts and Telegraphs, found me one day deep in pasting and cutting and when he got an explanation from me he firmly forbade any further immoral trafficking of this kind.

We so loved writing letters that we took on pen-friends in the States which we got out of missionary magazines, and one of mine sent me a present of a subscription to a magazine called *The American Girl* which gave us glimpses of the New World. This was heady material showing trendy clothes and an outlook on life as fresh as our own and fresher. I loved it so much that I wrote to the editor to tell him so and he published my letter with four words under it, my name and Blackrock, Ireland; then the letters began to come in earnest. They came from all over the States, from Alaska to Hawaii and although the address was meagre they somehow arrived, with just an occasional one coming via Louth or Cork, which also have a Blackrock. I now led a dream life sorting out all the letters looking for pen-friends, the junk mail, letters from ethnic societies, business agencies and religious associations and I saved all the exotic stamps and graciously presented people with pen-friends. Blackrock post office had to handle the deliveries as a matter of duty. I never really recovered from the episode, feeling a small optimistic glow whenever I saw a postman for years afterwards.

We then decided it was time we produced a literary magazine and so we published the *Girls' Monthly Gazette* and had great hopes of it becoming as well known as *Dublin Opinion*, calling ourselves the joint-editors just in case. Our magazine contained stories of uneven quality, beauty and cookery articles, an agony column which was my preserve, some verse and some advertisements illustrated by ourselves. We produced about a dozen a month, all handwritten in the privacy of my friend's bicycle room, and about half the copies were sold and the remaining ones lent at a reading fee. After several months the labour-intensive nature of the project caught up with us and we regretfully had to announce that publication of the *Girls' Monthly Gazette* would be suspended until further notice.

WE HAD NO BUS FARES to work on and no loose change or surplus pocket money, as we cycled to school. It was therefore difficult to save, as the demands on the allowance were many, but I had heard at home about post office savings schemes and resolved to stop being a spendthrift and open an account towards purchasing a large stamp album. My friend was instantly enthusiastic and we went down to the post office to take the decisive step. The postmistress opened two accounts in crisp beige covered books, with pages marked with wavy green lines to discourage fraud, and a system of sixpenny stamps affixed to little squares, and we left with a flourish, seeing new vistas opening before us. About an hour afterwards I began to regret the new departure. My weekly sixpence was now disposed of in the vaults of the post office and the week yawned before me without my having any visible means of support. After some deliberation I decided to close the account and withdraw my capital, but alas, there was a catch in it. In order to do this it was necessary to take out a minimum of two stamps; I would have no further capital for a whole week. However, my friend was a little better off and offered to lend me her back-up sixpence. I returned to the post office and bought a second stamp, waited a dignified interval of twenty minutes outside and then went in again, withdrew my savings, closed the account and gave my friend back her sixpence. The postmistress was beside herself with rage.

The routes to school were sources of interest and adventure. In hot weather we had a large number of tar bubbles to burst and we kept special little wooden spears for the job. The smell of the tar was addictive and we constantly ruined our shoes bending down and squidging bubbles wherever we spied fresh tar. People working the routes were also of interest. The Johnston Mooney and O'Brien horse-drawn bread-van stood somewhere along Sydney Avenue each day as we cycled by, and for some reason we were deadly enemies of the breadman. Snow came in its time and one day we were picking our way past the Johnston Mooney horse and van, and saw that the enemy was busy in at the door of a house with a delivery, and therefore out of the way. We wondered whether we would raise a laugh for ourselves somehow and we decided to throw a snowball at the horse to see if he would jump or even twitch a little. With one eye on the breadman and one on the snow we prepared a few snowballs and lobbed them at the unoffending horse. We were quite taken aback by the result. The horse reared up on his hind legs, the doors of the bread-van flew open and out tumbled all the trays of bread into the snow with a great clatter of wood upon wood. The breadman came tearing out, yelling expressions at us of which we had never heard the like before and we made off, panic-stricken. Not by any means natural cowards and game to take a risk in most circumstances, this was somewhat too much for us to sort out. We were very contrite about the horse, realising that we had taken advantage of our position in life as free-moving creatures but we were also sorry that we could never again linger near him. This horse was well known as the one under which an older girl in the district had climbed as a dare, and for some time we had been screwing up our courage to emulate her . Now we would never be able to do so.

THERE WAS A SMALL SHOP at the end of Sydney Terrace which kept us enthralled. Packed into its window were items of jewellery and junk, fans, statuettes, beaded evening bags which had seen better days, books, vases and sundry bric-a-brac. We stopped outside this shop every day and leaned over the handlebars of the bicycles to gaze in at the treasure trove, while the old lady who owned the shop stared out at us suspiciously. When Christmas loomed we went in every day pricing items suitable as presents, and then going out to review our present-buying budgets. We took the process seriously, quite unaware of the old lady's mounting dislike. One day we went in and she told us not to come in any more as we were always pricing things and we never bought anything. We were mortally offended by this rebuff and found being 'barred' an insurmountable humiliation. Christmas was almost upon us and all our planning had been for nothing, and the items in the window looked even more tantalising than before. So we devised a plan whereby the old dear would realise that all the power in life was not necessarily hers.

We decided to write to her and tell her that her shop was not all that great, and sign the letter 'The Phantom' for complete anonymity. This sinister plan afforded us much relief and that evening we composed the letter and met secretly to push it through the letter-box, feeling that justice had been done. We returned to our respective homes triumphant but I had a phone call from a shaken collaborator that night; it had crossed the mind of my friend that we might actually be connected with the letter in the mind of the old lady. It was agreed that we meet early the next morning and act out a plan she had devised to recover the situation. We would get back the letter unopened in the following way: If we waited hidden until she arrived and opened her door and went in, we could then rush in together, although we had been barred, one of us could price something and bring her anger yet again on our heads while the other dropped her books all over the floor and scooped up the letter with them. It was risky but it could save us from jail or even worse.

We waited motionless nearby the next morning and carried out the plan as laid. I had the effrontery to whirl into the shop, my heart in my mouth, and as the flabbergasted shopowner turned round I priced something while my friend dropped her books all over the floor, grabbed up the letter with them and made for the door. I was bawled out by the old lady and, much shaken but victorious, we left her in a state of absolute confusion. Fearing repercussions, we used an alternative route to school for a long time afterwards. It was becoming practically impossible to make the daily journeys without fear of being arrested.

Christmas came and we had to buy our presents elsewhere. It was the hardest winter in memory and as we trudged each day towards education we took to passing the shop once more out of boredom. The window was still packed with exciting items, a change of bric-a-brac since Christmas, and we felt sad about being barred. We decided to snow the old lady out of her shop, thinking that if we posted enough snow through the letter-box she wouldn't be able to get in. We set about the operation silently and purposefully. The job completed, we left, elated at our originality, and we arranged to dash past the following morning to see how she liked being locked out. So, early next day we came stealthily by, woollen pixies covering our faces for disguise, and to our great surprise we saw her sweeping waves of water out of the shop. It had never occurred to us that the snow would melt overnight.

After that we left her strictly alone, thinking that the situation was sure to rebound in some unpleasant manner, but we were occasionally tempted to check on her. One day we found the shop closed and dark in the afternoon. The jewellery and finery were still there but there was no sign of the old lady. We bought a few sweets in a neighbouring shop to try and pick up some intelligence and learned that she had died the previous evening; now we felt really sad and ashamed, for we had no way of expiating our guilt and would have to live with our remorse, for we thought we had sent her to her death by our attentions. Maybe we were lonely for the feud too.

WE WENT TO A convent school which was run by an enclosed order in the district. The convent buildings dated from various eras but it was the original cloister which fascinated us. It was a tall, dark, damp-looking place with small windows high up in the walls and heavy trees waving their branches over at it. At the word 'cloister' we shivered with mystery, as this was somewhere we could never penetrate unless we eventually joined the order, something which we considered highly unlikely. My friend and I used to creep through the shrubbery after school and gaze in fascination at this building, repeating slowly to frighten ourselves, 'Once they go in, they can never come out, never come out, never, never, never ...' until we practically screamed. The matter of enclosure became almost an obsession with us and if we saw a nun on the driveway anywhere near the front gates, we would engage her in conversation, moving slowly towards the gates in the hopes that she would inadvertently step over the threshold and, to our minds, break her enclosure. We were sure there would be a horrifically splendid spectacle and could imagine the poor creature realising what had happened, running around in circles in terror, screaming and crying and then setting off down Merrion Avenue she knew not where, for we were convinced that once a toe went outside the boundary line and the enclosure was broken, the nun could never, ever come back in again.

Occasionally one of the nuns had to go to town to see a doctor, and whenever such a journey was necessary the white horse in the field behind the laundry was hitched to the cab that was kept in the farm buildings. Then, two or three nuns travelled together along the Merrion Road at a pace not exactly suited to urgent cases for surgery. We presumed that the doctor would have to come out to the cab to examine the patient, otherwise the nun's foot would have to touch the ground and the enclosure would be broken. We asked one of them who had made the trip whether she had tried to leap out of the cab when it came to a halt somewhere and were most disappointed to learn that nuns always said their prayers as they went along and never looked out at all.

We did not think that nuns did anything so worldly as eating and we thought they must sleep standing up, as they wore heavy semi-circular veils in which they could never have lain down on a bed. We never considered they might take them off, as visualising a nun in bed was too much for even our vivid imaginations. The veils did not turn with their heads and in order to speak to someone beside them they had to do a ninety-degree swoop, which meant a slight time lag in conversation, rather like a two-way radio.

Our school was the first in Ireland to implement the Montessori method of educating children. This method, devised by

Maria Montessori to rehabilitate under-privileged children in the streets of Naples and develop their capabilities, was greeted with the greatest of interest and the programme was watched by educationalists throughout Ireland. Children went to Montessori school as early as four years of age and my sister even started at three. This meant that no other form of education outside the home could possibly have affected us and we were sealed off in a brave new world of our own. If the method is to be evaluated fully it might be said that it had a huge influence in helping us to form relationships, for the Montessori message was that the world and all the people in it were for investigating in a positive way.

Nowadays, everyone is familiar with innovative educational methods, but at this time such thinking broke new areas in a dramatic way. Freedom of movement for the children was advocated, creativity was top of the pops and education was expected to come in all forms, with tactile skills being developed by means of frames for buttoning, tying tapes, bricks for building, insets for identifying shapes, drawing and painting, modelling, as well as reading, writing and counting, altogether a varied and enjoyable programme. I could read well at four and borrowed the reader from the class above because I had finished my own and was bored with it. The means to acquire all these skills were spread before us, with children who had been buttoning their own coats for a year or so being introduced to buttoning on a frame, but the emphasis was on the development of the exploratory and creative instincts of every child.

Freedom of movement meant that we walked and ran about wherever we liked, or rushed up to the teacher and walloped her for attention, if we thought we knew the answer to a question. We raced ahead with reading, writing and spelling and since we rarely applied ourselves to anything in particular for very long, our arithmetic was just about all right. We had our own percussion band and to every child's way of thinking, it was just terrific being at school. Everyone smiled on us benignly and although Madame Montessori had not had our kind of child in mind when she devised her methods, we took to the system with gusto. Inspectors and visitors came to gaze on us as we brought in birds' nests, learned to use a knitting nancy and then to knit and make greeting cards for all the feasts on the calendar. We were taken on nature walks in the convent gardens and often lightened the proceedings by shinning up trees and perching aloft, to try the mettle of some unfortunate teacher who could not quite decide where creativity ended and wild behaviour began. Life was one long picnic as we moved from class to class, and high spirits were the order of the day. It was only when we reached the top class in the junior school at the ripe age of ten or so that we encountered discipline by being given some authority and it was enjoyable to meet and savour responsibility for the first time in the form of special tasks. Generously allowed to combine creativity with special responsibilities, we rejoiced in this new extension of living.

What I did not know – what we all did not know – was the great culture shock that awaited us Montessori chickens when we went across to secondary school. It came like a thunderclap in the first year, but in the manner of thunderclaps it was not really registered as something which had come to stay. The storm followed in the second year as the realities of life began to dawn on us. In the first year we had continued to tear from our desks in excitement and thump the teachers if we had the answer, and we had chatted gaily through class in spite of repeated correction, rising from our desks and strolling around the room to stretch our legs if the need arose. Our attitude was that of mini-adults enjoying a new phase in our educational life and we still had the upper hand through our sheer self-confidence, without realising it or realising why. No teacher could get through to us and no one thought of sitting down to evaluate our behaviour. We had been at the school since we were about four years of age, but our astonishing demeanour for secondary school girls was a mystery to everyone, and naturally we were totally bewildered by the new system to which we were expected to conform immediately. Here we were, prime products of an educational system specifically designed to awaken us on every level, one which had even eschewed memorising on the premise that it might block our exploratory urges, and no one could make head nor tail of us.

When introduced to French we embraced it laughingly. 'Derrière la maison de Monsieur Desgranges, il y a un très joli jardin où Denise et Marcel jouent souvent' held no terrors for us and we lapped up Denise and Marcel's adventures and begged for more, acting out their rôles unasked. We clowned around the classroom imitating French accents, brought in postcards of Paris sent by friends of our parents and begged our mothers for the box of 'Evening in Paris' scent widely popular at the time, because it had a picture of the Tour Eiffel on it. We even called one another 'Mademoiselle' for Frenchiness and thought the business of learning a Continental language was great sport altogether.

The Irish class was treated in somewhat similar style. To absorb all this wild energy the Irish teacher wisely let us do a play and so we pranced about the stage acting out the story of 'Ordóigín', or 'Tom Thumb', and enjoying immensely our first encounter with drama. We rehearsed in the concert hall and spent a lot of the time having adventures under the actual stage, rather than on it, as we had found access to the nether regions by trapdoor. Here we descended with torches in our mouths and found a veritable treasure trove of coins, pens, brooches and sundry items which had fallen down through the wide cracks in the boards for countless years. No one could understand how the members of the cast waiting to go on were often dirty and elated when called on stage. Next we mastered a play in French about Joan of Arc and stunned ourselves and everyone else by giving polished performances. I was the Dauphin and when I was sitting on my throne, splendidly attired in cloth of gold ordering everyone about, it was discovered that my feet did not reach the floor. An upholstered box had to be fetched to give me full authority as I sent one of my friends to death on the scaffold in her rôle of Joan. At twelve or thirteen years of age, we put on a full-length performance of *Hamlet* and regarded it as great fun.

We also had a French club which met once a month, on which occasions we were meant to give an invited audience a lecture in French. Although we were young at twelve years of age to be addressing strangers in another language, we thought the whole idea was first-class and took to it with the usual enthusiasm. I chose music for my subject and organised my friend to illustrate my text with snatches of French songs, 'La Vie en Rose' for the section about cabaret, rounding off with a rousing rendition of 'La Marseillaise' to show that there was plenty of spirit about, in case anyone thought otherwise. I heard years afterwards that the audience had had to cough into their handkerchiefs to contain their laughter.

The end to this career of self-determination, to this embracing of creativity, to this love of life and one-man-band outlook came in our second year, with the arrival of new blood in the form of boarders and some day students from other schools. The boarders were the catalyst. The majority of these girls were fresh from primary national schools where the teachers would not have stood for any nonsense. These girls were beautifully fluent in Irish, we were not, as ours was east-coast Irish taught to us by east-coast adults. The boarders were quiet, obedient, brilliant at Irish and well ahead in mathematics. They absorbed the new disciplines of algebra and geometry without any difficulty, as they brought to them the concentration bred of years of discipline and they offered no resistance whatsoever to the new learning processes. For years they had learned by memorising and they could commit large chunks of poetry to memory without any strain. The 'freagra' they put at the end of every calculation was invariably correct. They sat politely in their desks, were all right-handed and had no immediate home influence with which to challenge the teachers. By contrast, we were hooligans. Unless we were interested in what we were doing we lacked concentration, and black clouds began to gather over what had once been a sunlit, if totally unrealistic existence for girls of our age. Nevertheless, we got on very well with the boarders, exchanging skills by doing their French for them while they did our maths, and sometimes we did messages for them or brought them in something interesting to eat from home.

So, for many reasons, the boarders were 'in' and we were

'out'. The newcomers were regarded as the 'real' people of the school and we were the intruders, having intruded, that is, from the age of four. It was a sobering and deeply affecting experience and one which was to have far-reaching effects on our lives. To have been the toast of the town and then to find you are bewilderingly *non grata* is one of life's great shocks, but facing it at such a young age made it quite traumatic. We were deeply and lastingly offended and the sad part of it was that no one realised what was happening to us, or understood the effect of the rejection on us. We were in for discipline without relationship and we knew it.

I should have liked to have been able to tell in class about my own culture once I recognised it, the kind of people I came from and how they earned their living from one generation to the next, but no one would have found it the least bit interesting in this new-wave period, since the rural background was regarded as more Irish and therefore infinitely superior. I thought it of interest that my father's people had lived in the same house in Harold's Cross from 1909, that they had been church sculptors and painters and that one of them had worked on the famous statue of 'The Dead Christ' by Hogan under the high altar in the Carmelite Church in Clarendon Street in Dublin. My father had told me how he remembered his father taking him down to the North Mall in 1913 during the Great Lock-Out, to see the sodality men turning back Catholic children who were being sent over to Liverpool to be properly fed by workers' families there. I knew that my grandfather had defended Dreyfus to a large crowd in Dublin and had been remembered thereafter by the Jewish community; how the same grandfather had attended the Royal University and how he practised his shorthand for college lectures by taking down sermons at Mass under his hat and writing them up word for word when he got home. There was much of interest in all our backgrounds but there was no room for it in our education system.

OUR SELF-CONFIDENCE began to show the damage in direct ratio to the lack of understanding on the part of those responsible for it, and we involuntarily fell into a state of constant warfare with the authorities. Without really wishing to do so, we committed ourselves to a course of disruptive behaviour, for what we wanted was a recognition of ourselves as ourselves, as worthwhile beings, but no one recognised our unconscious demands for affection and attention, apart from one or two good souls who did not have a direct bearing on our training. Our parents did not know anything much about our activities at school beyond paying our fees and checking occasionally as to what subjects we were studying. We would have been mortified if they had, but it was long before the time when this would become popular in the form of parent-teacher meetings. Had our French Resistance Movement type of behaviour come to light, we might have become unpopular at home as well as at school. It was a hopeless muddle and I constantly asked to be sent away to boarding school as I thought that this would be the answer to it all. I had read glowing accounts of English boarding schools complete with dormitory feasts and nightly haunting of ruins in the school grounds, and I thought I was missing out on things on every side.

We astonished even ourselves with our waywardness. We smoked in class, put on the blackboard an eel which had been collected on the seashore at lunchtime and threw water-bombs at each other and some out of the windows. We used a blackboard on wheels during choir practice which had a space of about eighteen inches between the board and the floor, and my bosom friend used to cling to the back of it and conduct the choir behind the teacher's back with a lisle-stockinged leg. She always kept perfect tempo and exactly at the end of each song the leg would be withdrawn and we would be reduced to inexplicable and uncontrollable laughter. Confusion and condemnation reigned.

On one occasion I inadvertently flicked ink down the back of a nun's light-coloured habit when I was waving my pen about and I neither slept nor ate for days while I was waiting for the axe to fall, sure that it would be traced back to me. It never occurred to me to tell her and save myself a lot of anxiety. I preferred to wither away. Opening gymslip buttons was a fun occupation as the gymslips had shoulder flaps to allow the garment have a lower hemline as its wearer grew taller. The buttons would be opened from behind at precisely the same time so that the wearer's gymslip fell down to her waist. No sooner had she rebuttoned one side when the girl behind her would undo it again. She could be reduced to a state of panic if a third girl removed her belt as well, while she was struggling with the shoulders, and this process was kept for special occasions when we indulged in over-the-top giddiness.

One evening after school, when the boarders had gone to their study and the nuns to their prayers and we should have been at home, we brought our bicycles into the junior school through a window. We started by cycling all around downstairs and, becoming bored with this, we brought the bicycles upstairs. This afforded better opportunities for excitement and so we lined them up at the end of the top corridor and got ready for a spectacular ride. We flew along the corridor getting up a nice momentum and then took off down the stairs, still upright in spite of the turn in the staircase, down a further staircase and along a tiled corridor, through the foyer, down a shallow staircase into the assembly hall and a few times around it to reduce speed and do a victory lap, rather than land in a heap of metal and person in front of the statue of Saint Joseph, who, indeed, would have been surprised at nothing we did.

WE HAD GREAT DIFFICULTY as regards the learning of Irish. The situation is more understandable if we go back one generation, as we were of the generation following the one which had been caught up in the Irish revival. During those years, dazed grandmothers had wheeled out grandchildren with names incomprehensible to them such as Sorcha, Gobnait and Caoimhe, a far cry from the Emilies, Marjories and Stanleys to whom they had expected to relate as grandparents. The cultural changeover had been tremendous and a new generation had warmly embraced a whole new set of values without having to undertake much in the way of obligations attached to them. Compulsory Irish and compulsory qualification in it for third level education had not arrived in our parents' generation, it came with ours. In the 1940s the great change in values was brought about by the establishment of the new educated native Irish Catholic middle class, which now staffed government offices and semi-state bodies.

It was the time when Celtic designs proliferated, appearing on the covers of our copybooks, on the covers and sides of text books and even curling around pencils. Some of these designs were very suitable for idlers to extend, fill in, duplicate and trace and were always used for such entertainment. By government decree the words *Déanta in Éirinn* were stamped on all items manufactured in the newly industrialising Ireland and even imported goods bore their country of origin in Irish, such as *an tSualainn tír a dhéanta*, or *Déanta sa tSeapáin* which was stamped on the bottoms of leprechauns made in Tokyo. The thrust for Irish as first language was overpowering. My father was a tireless enthusiast for the language as he had learned it while working in An Gúm, the Irish language publications section, as a civil servant. He had rejoiced in this opportunity to learn the language, but he did not ask us to speak Irish at home as he believed that a command of English as our first language would be more useful in the Europe of tomorrow.

An unbelievable drawback to our learning Irish was that our grammars were also written in Irish. This meant that we were learning a language we did not yet know through a language we did not yet know and although the Department of Education may have thought this was a way of looping the loop, *Gramadach Mhic Léighinn* was almost a total mystery to some of us, as was *Cúrsaí an Lae*. When the boarders joined us the teachers were naturally delighted to have mellifluous Irish spoken in class, as they had a chance to brush up their own command, and we were left like bus stops on the road to fluency. To our minds our texts were of a dullness which made them well-nigh unopenable. *Séadhna, Jimín Mháire Thaidhg* and *Peig* were characters so far from our culture that they failed to hold our interest. Peig lived on an island, smoked a clay pipe and, according to the illustrations in our book, wore men's boots and a sack around her waist. Séadhna sat by the fire and pulled on his pipe, only removing it to say 'fadó, fadó', before he lapsed back into silence, gazing into the coals for inspiration; and Jimín Mháire Thaidhg wore no shoes at all and spent his time skipping around the bog. Don Quixote in Irish was well nigh incomprehensible to us and we could just about take *M'Asal Beag Dubh*, but we hungered for interesting stories. There was nothing snobbish in our attitude, we just wanted a good story like the ones we had in French, *Pêcheurs d'Islande* and others. We couldn't identify with the Irish texts.

Misery without drama is not of interest to young people and those who chose our Irish texts could not have known much about growing minds, and probably acted out of a love of literature without realising that they were not passing it on to us. We were found to be gravely at fault for not gobbling up all this lore and we wished that we could wake up one morning and find that we were miraculously excellent at Irish and could henceforth lead a charmed existence. We were expected to feel ashamed at our lack of enthusiasm for Irish, but this only deepened our feelings of inferiority and compacted the problem. It was obligatory that we pass Irish in order to go to university and it is a fact that I went through school making enthusiastic progress in four other languages and just got by in Irish.

Groans were expressed as we sat down each weekend to write our Irish essays. The tactic most widely used was the sprinkling of such compositions with Irish proverbs and blessings. Magnanimous phrases such as 'The blessings of one generation be on the next' would lead off the work and slightly irrelevant observations such as 'There is no hearth like your own' would find their way into the story to swell its size. Morbid warnings about faithless behaviour after the mode of the proverbs would appear in Irish in every essay and cosy sayings would be inserted here and there, whether or not they were apposite. Wisdom abounded, all gleaned from school texts down the years and carefully collected for this purpose.

We would emerge triumphant from writing a four-page Irish essay having filled the required norm.

In boys' schools there was a further complication as regards the learning of Irish, particularly with the Christian Brothers. Teachers were often transferred from one school to another around the country and this could have a painful effect. A teacher with Munster Irish would be replaced by one with Donegal or Connaught Irish and the carefully learned pronunciation of yesterday would be supplanted by a whole set of new sounds. For many of us the learning of Irish was a nightmare, recurring long after we had left school, and dreaming that you had failed Irish in the Leaving Certificate and were therefore good for nothing was quite a common experience.

Gaeltacht colleges helped towards a final solution to the Irish problem and those who spent a year there between preparatory and senior school beat the system. I begged to go, but there was so much going on already at home in the field of education that my parents did not consider it necessary. The few weeks we spent there one summer convinced us that it was a great place, with lots of new friends and a céilí every night when we hopped around learning set dances like the Walls of Limerick. Boss of the college was the Fear Mór, a huge man who acted as a delicious threat as he abhorred any speaking of English on the premises. In the afternoons we would stream off to Baile na nGall or Fail na Stocaí to swim and watch the boys playing hurling on the strand. There was no feeling here of 'not being right for the part' and we even began to like Irish, taken as we were as children of an alien culture who had come to learn the language and were expected to enjoy themselves in the process. We were taught how to play the tin whistle and to sing in Irish and we loved this action-packed programme.

WE PARTICULARLY LOVED learning Irish dancing which we did at school and coming up to competition time we went into town to Miss Medlar's dancing school in Adelaide Road for extra tuition. Miss Medlar herself taught us, a birdy little woman who loved children and was a brilliant teacher. We would get into dancing pumps and float around the floor like thistledown, doing the slip jig, the double jig and various reels. Then we would change into loud clackety shoes and practise the double hornpipe, 'St Patrick's Day' and the Blackbird until we danced ourselves into a trance, loving the indomitable rhythms. My sister won the coveted Champion's Cup when she was twelve. Her rival was a Basque girl who was a good Irish dancer but the winning power lay in the slip jig, for my sister realised that she was the lighter of the two. When the final of the competition was being fought out she donned her pumps and set off across the floor, executing a slip jig that would have shamed a jinni-go-up for its lightness as she tipped the parquet here and there, a pure exercise in levitation, and joy of joys, the cup was awarded to her, a milestone in life, as Irish dancing tuition ended when we crossed over to the senior school.

Whenever we were in Miss Medlar's school, we were torn with longing to be included in the tap dancing class. Until then we had thought it was only for children in films or pantomimes, something a bit doubtful or glitzy and not in our stream of culture, but we saw those children with beautiful black patent shoes with steel tips on them and heard the joyous rhythmic beat and we pleaded and begged at home to take it up too. Alas, our pleas fell on deaf ears as the prevailing culture load was considered to be adequate.

ACROSS THE ROAD from school was a grind establishment run by a jovial ex-schoolteacher called Willie Martin. Mr Martin's academy was the answer to a lot of people's problems. Young people who had learning difficulties, one or two who had been expelled from school, some with problems at home, occasionally someone with impaired hearing and those of us who wanted supplementary teaching in maths or Irish after school and had persuaded our parents to fund it in the form of a grind, all happily crossed the road into Martin's and had every tear wiped away.

Willie Martin was the original fat jolly man and we loved

him. He had an invalid wife and several children and he lived on Cross Avenue in a tall terraced house which had been converted into classrooms. An odd time Willie did not make it into class and could be seen crossing the top landing in check dressing-gown, looking straight ahead and not getting involved with anyone, and on such a day we would find the work all set up on the blackboard. Because we loved him we would settle down immediately and do our work as well as we could for the next class we had with him.

Mr Martin's secret was that he loved us. He would shout at us, call us ruffians and ask us why we had ever been born and then he would give a big chuckle and shake his head slowly, taking away all the tensions built up by feeling inferior about maths and Irish, or whatever was troubling us. He would explain a point clearly, slamming out the information in a way that your attention just could not wander and then check to see that everyone knew what he was on about before he finished up. If you didn't know, you spoke up, he explained it to you all over again and miracle of miracles, you had it for good. He would call out the examples of the problems you were to do in class, saying 'Page forty-three, number two, five, eight, eleven and thirteen, have you them done?' all in one sentence and we would laugh each time and then settle into doing them and possibly get them right. When it came to Irish he would read it through in his beautiful melodious voice, making sure we listened to every word and then go back and translate it for us. If your mind wandered he would stare at you over his glasses and maybe pull a face at you to bring you back. This blend of teaching and teasing was an unbelievable boon. Most of the time he held to strict discipline but you could never be sure when he would catch your eye and give an approving smile of encouragement. Meals used to be brought in to him on trays during class, and he would munch through a crispy fry and pour himself several cups of tea and down them without missing a beat.

A distinct advantage of going to Willie Martin's academy was that it was a co-educational establishment. The boys were just as thrilled about this as we were and before we went in we would tighten our plastic belts to nip in the waists of gym-slips, remove our hated ties and turn the collars of our blouses up in order to look a cut above schoolgirls. Moran's French Grammar came in useful as lipstick, as it had a red cover, which it was sufficient to lick and then kiss in order to transfer a nice red glow to the lips. Hair was combed forward like film-stars and we were ready for the exciting world of Martin's, even managing to make dates for walks down the pier during the summer term and a trip or two to the Adelphi and Pavil-ion cinemas in Dún Laoghaire as well.

One of my brothers got a mediocre Intermediate Certifi-cate and then idled the following year so he appeared to be heading for a less than mediocre Leaving Certificate. My mother packed him off to Willie Martin's academy rather than see him pass an idyllic summer, so that he could enrol for the matriculation examination and maybe get one or two subjects which he could keep toward the following year. Mr Martin shouted at him and cajoled him, along with the other summer students, and insisted that they all do a spot of work in the summer evenings, as well as meeting girls. September eventu-ally came and they all sat for the 'matric' and a couple of weeks later Mr Martin rang up to tell him that he had got all five subjects in the examination. He now had his university entrance secured and all thanks to Willie Martin who knew how to join brains to curriculum.

A further advantage of attendance at Martin's was that in addition to specific courses paid for, we were allowed to at-tend any class we liked if time permitted. So, going home in the evening you might find that you now knew all about the making of Germany or the coastline of the Mediterranean, as well as Irish and maths. Those of us who frequented Martin's never mentioned the matter at school and Mr Martin's tuition was complementary rather than in opposition. The system worked for us and we worked the system.

AT HOME, OUR SOURCES of knowledge were many but the most accessible and most frequently used asset was a full set of the *Concise Universal Encyclopaedia*, published in the 1930s

71

by the Amalgamated Press of London. My father had bought the copies month by month and had had them bound in hard covers, and the full set was split into four volumes entitled A-CAR, CAR-HIL, HIL-POM, and POM-Z. These volumes were great for homework as they had splendid maps and biographies and succinct summaries of subjects of history and geography, and I thought no home was without them, so much so that I once told a teacher who questioned me about it that my information came from HIL-POM.

School reports came at Christmas, Easter and the beginning of the summer and these were controlled by my sister who could detect nuns' handwriting at any distance. There was a report inspection and correction session held every few months, when the envelope containing the school reports was extracted from the post and put aside for treatment with steaming kettle and knife in the old comedy postmistress style. We absolutely had to know what was in the reports before they reached our parents and we never considered the 'treating' of reports in any way reprehensible. Our kitchen offered superb laboratory conditions for dealing with the reports, as it could be closed off from the rest of the house. A day would be chosen when there were no parents about, a scout would be posted and the implements would be spread on the kitchen table. My sister was a highly skilled counterfeiter and she used Polar White, a kitchen bleach, to whiten out offending figures, and a variety of inks for matching. Great care was taken not to wrinkle the paper, working with cotton wool and tweezers and the white correcting ink from my father's desk. Friends gathered in the kitchen with their reports and when all was accomplished, tea and biscuits were served as we celebrated the work. All anxiety over the reports had been banished and they were safely sealed back in their envelopes in which they would join the post on the morrow and life would go on as usual.

I had a passion for mending and fixing things and even spent some of my pocket money on magic mending substances in tubes called 'Torcement' and 'Araldite'. Once when my father's cigar burnt a hole in the back of my mother's new tweed coat at the theatre, I stayed up half the night mending it invisibly with strands from the inside seams and unexpectedly earned the huge sum of a pound from my grateful father. As a fixer-upper I danced back and forth across the line existing between being helpful and just enjoying mending for its own sake. My mending jobs often came apart but I would buy a new type of adhesive and start all over again. I even tried to mend a lovely Waterford cut-glass bowl which I broke making jelly-fuzz, so broken-hearted was I by the accident.

An old copy of *Pears Cyclopaedia* was another source of information and we loved reading it, particularly the sections on dress which gave sound advice. It recommended keeping a special set of stays for housework, with the instructions 'When dressing for housework, put your two hands deep within your stays and lift up the surplus flesh over the top of them. In this way it will be possible to move about more comfortably and do the housework more efficiently'. The section on illness and disease was more sobering and the entry under 'cancer' was often read by my mother who had a dread of ever getting it.

MONTHLY PERIODICALS which came into our home apart from *Dublin Opinion* were the *Irish Tatler and Sketch* and *Social and Personal*. Weekly we had *The Listener*, *Life* magazine and *The Saturday Evening Post* from America. All this reading matter was passed around and absorbed with interest and often avidly discussed. *The National Geographic Magazine* was bought frequently and always ended up in one of the window seats in the study. The *Tatler and Sketch* kept us up to the moment on fashionable weddings in Donnybrook and Haddington Road and my parents appeared in it occasionally at diplomatic and other functions. It also gave details of people who went off to Rome to be married as was the fashion, and sometimes reported people 'spending their honeymoon touring the west of Ireland'. Hunt balls were reported in detail and country high life was always fascinating to read about. The advertisements in these society magazines featured ladies in high fashion long leather or silk gloves, with arms outstretched to demonstrate their elegance. We particularly liked the advertisements for Pond's Cold Cream. There were also advertisements for foundation garments and other feminine secrets and a good motoring diary prevented the magazines from getting entirely into the hands of the women. *The Listener* balanced out all this frivolity and my father studied it each week as part of his work in Radio Éireann. *Life* magazine kept us firmly in the twentieth century and *The Saturday Evening Post* brought us glimpses of the New World with its breezy cartoons and fresh American humour. We got the *Irish Independent* and *The Irish Times* newspapers each day. At that time the three daily papers, which included the *Irish Press*, had such distinct personalities that you could guess what newspaper someone read after five minutes conversation with them.

Comics were neither encouraged nor discouraged at home and we sometimes bought them out of pocket money. *The Champion, Hotspur, The Wizard* and *Film Fun* were hot favourites. We begged and borrowed *The Dandy* and *The Beano* from friends and very occasionally bought a new one for ourselves. They were fun but so quickly read that it seemed a pity to spend pocket money on them. Nonetheless our conversations were sometimes peppered with allusions to Desperate Dan and his Aunt Aggie, Keyhole Kate, Snitch and Snatch and other comic folk. We adopted their language and addressed each other with expressions such as 'byrrrrrh', 'garn', 'doggonit', 'ug', 'tysk, tysk', 'gnerrsh' and 'psssst'. *Girls' Crystal* was a weekly magazine supplied to me by my friend when she had finished with it and I can still recall the delight of getting my head down into the adventures of women pilots, who 'moistened their nether lip' as they prepared to effect a nose dive into the jungle.

WE LISTENED TO 'Drawing and Painting with Marion King' on Radio Éireann every week. Marion King would relate stories about Séan Bunny, Glicín Buí and other characters of her imagination and give clear instructions about materials and techniques of drawing and painting. Prizes of the order of half a crown and five shillings were awarded and the competition entries were rolled in newspaper and labelled clearly before being posted to the GPO in which Radio Éireann was housed.

Marion was aware that not all parents could afford painting materials for their children and she encouraged competitors to make their own. One method was to use the ash from turf and mix it with water, leave it to set in bottle tops and use it with water-colour brushes. This produced a range of colours from white to darkest brown through all the shades of cream, beige, rust and fawn. Marion then gave tips on adding further colours.

The excitement of winning a prize on the programme was tremendous. It meant having your name called out on the radio as well as receiving a sum of money, and we entered every week and often won prizes. I once won a hand-made long-legged mouse doll made by Marion herself, for her dedication to the programme was such that in the absence of a budget she made the prizes at home. When Caltex had a great idea and began to run children's art competitions, the papers presented the venture as art for children for the first time in Ireland. My father was most upset on Marion's account but her crisp reply was, 'If it's the right thing, Mr Kelly, it doesn't matter who does it'.

6

Music

MUSIC WAS VERY IMPORTANT in our lives. Everyone in our generation was exposed to music, and music radio programmes were important, as were the concerts given by the Radio Éireann Symphony Orchestra in the Phoenix Hall, which were open to the public. The symphony concerts had previously been given in the Capitol Theatre on Sunday afternoons and our parents attended them regularly, bringing some of us with them. A box was always reserved for my father and we thought that this was rather grand. We were expected to read the programme carefully and to know the soloists' names and, to a lesser extent, the composers of the works played. We liked going to the concerts and we used to bend forward and clap extravagantly like the people in films to make up for having to sit still during the performance. The glamour of it all was well worth the strain and sometimes the music was so nice that we forgot to be bored and just enjoyed it instead. Terry O'Connor was the leader of the orchestra and we watched her closely, amazed that a woman should control all those men.

Piano lessons were a must for every child and although

some would have preferred to have learnt elocution and have been able to recite, the piano it had to be. We first learnt from a private teacher in Blackrock who had been trained by the Reid School of Music. This school was famous for its attention to 'touch' and the gentle lift to the wrist could be detected immediately a Reid school pupil began to play. Our teacher was a melancholy woman who lived alone in a huge house called 'Laurel Hill' on the way into Blackrock. The drawing-room where she gave lessons was over-furnished, dark and very dreary and we passed the time waiting for lessons by counting the pictures and prints on the crammed walls. She didn't like any of us apart from one brother who had no special promise as a pianist, and he was the one who got excellent reports. He continued to hold her approval without any apparent growth in musicality until one day he stood on the piano stool at home and drew a moustache and crossed eyes on the bust of Beethoven; my parents realised that he was trying to tell them something and not long afterwards released him from a musical future. My father did a cartoon of it in *Dublin Opinion*.

Miss Hand and Miss Bonaparte Wyse were the other music teachers in the district. Miss Hand lived in a sunny chintzy house on Waltham Terrace with a pretty porch and a garden full of flowers. Children loved going to her for music lessons and it was easy to know why. She kept a chest of comics and sent no end-of-term bills but preferred the children to pay per lesson, so there were never any rows about not practising. No fee, no lesson. Full of self-confidence the children bounced in and out of Miss Hand's, slammed down their half-crown on the piano and set to. Always keen on doing surveys I accompanied a friend to her lesson and was quite bowled over by the jolly atmosphere. Miss Hand was a delightful person who didn't bother about clocks and watches and just stopped the lesson when the repertoire had been run through and the next pupil was arriving. She was known to cook her meals to music and would slip out and put on the peas for a Scarlatti sonata while a piece by Schumann marked 'Largo' was just the thing for doing the potatoes to a turn.

Miss Bonaparte Wyse, the other local teacher was a direct

descendant of Napoleon who, in his short and busy life can't have had much time for music lessons. The name lent mystique to the house in Sydney Avenue with its heavy dark bushes right up to the door. I did not succeed in penetrating the fastness of Miss Bonaparte Wyse as she taught adults rather than children and I couldn't pal up with any of those, but I did catch an occasional glimpse of her and decided that she looked very like Napoleon, if the picture in HIL-POM was anything to go by.

We eventually left 'Laurel Hill' and its gloom and headed for the Royal Irish Academy of Music, a group of brightly lit Georgian houses in Westland Row. Founded in 1856, it had a fine decorated entrance hall with a big coke fire glowing in a high grate for most of the year. A small fat man with round glasses stood with his back to it most of the time. He was called John and he was the porter and had his finger on the pulse of the Academy. The office was brisk and efficient and everything seemed to go on oiled wheels. Music lessons went on in every room, sending out a blare of sound, and arpeggios tore up and down keyboards while loud soprano screams came from distant rooms. A woman could have been attacked twice over and no one ever would have noticed her cries for help.

Our first teacher was Dina Copeman. Dina suffered much from the cold and she would sit in hat and coat in a tiny overheated room with huge hot pipes running through it, warming her hands at a two-bar electric fire on the table beside the piano. During the lessons my face used to get quite red on the side nearest the fire and it was hard to concentrate on scales with your ear about to melt and drop off. It was during one of our lessons that my sister and I witnessed a most thrilling scene.

I was at the piano and she was sitting waiting for her lesson when the door opened and a girl came in. It was one of Miss Copeman's prize pupils who had come to tell her that she no longer wished to pursue music as a career, and would rather take up something less strenuous. Dina let fly with all the pent-up grief and outrage of her Lithuanian forebears. The shouting could have been heard in Dalkey and the student stood there dumbfounded as she reproached her with all the care she had lavished on her brilliant career. We two sat turned to stone until, unnoticed by Dina in her agony, we gathered our music and our belongings and sneaked out of the room. Going home, we agreed it was just as well we wouldn't be taking music as a career, as we would never be a match for Dina in the case of a change of heart.

Dorothy Stokes taught theory and harmony in the Academy, and also piano. She was held in great affection and her full figure, with cigarette dangling from her lower lip and briefcase in hand, were part of the scene. There was a story in the Academy that she had once sent a child into a teacher next door to have the 'Pixies' Goodnight Song' played for her, as Dorothy said that she could not demonstrate the piece herself because you had to cross your hands on the keyboard the whole time in the piece and she couldn't get across her ample chest.

When I reached the intermediate section I had the good fortune to become a pupil of Rhona Marshall, who in turn had been a pupil of Edith Best, who was a pupil of Esposito, composer and professor of music at the Academy. I loved playing by ear but I promised my mother that I wouldn't do so and that I would learn to play the piano 'properly'. I really wanted to play freely and got into trouble for playing my brother's pieces in vamped up versions in different keys, but I gave that up and then rued it later when no one wanted to hear sonatas at parties. I set about resolving the sight-reading difficulties when we were once asked to prepare four new pieces over the Easter holidays. I chose four Bach pieces because the tempo never changed and the music was therefore much easier to sight-read than that of other composers. Mrs Marshall could hardly believe her ears on the resumption of term when I produced my Bach repertoire, as it wasn't so easy for teachers to interest their pupils in Bach and his contemporaries, and heads kept popping around the door all through my lesson to see the child who had learnt four Bach pieces by choice.

My first duet was with a live-wire pupil and although we practised in each others' houses at weekends, we spent most of the time consuming cakes and tea so that the first time we actually performed the repertoire for Mrs Marshall was at the Feis Cheoil itself. She had been a little dubious about letting us go ahead and play and she brought a wire recorder into our lesson to let us hear ourselves, but when she played it back all there was to be heard on the wire was her voice remonstrating in despair. Not at all daunted we went into the competition uninhibited by depression or competitiveness, and we played with such vigour and enthusiasm that we carried off second prize. Others who had practised dutifully for many weeks and whose parents had learnt the other part of the duet to play with them, were somewhat burned out. The adjudicator said we were good individual players, not really something you would look for in a duet, and as we sailed away with the award Mrs Marshall was truly at a loss for words. Still, she gave us our due because it was her policy to encourage everyone, and she was always pleased if her students were playing well and never minded about prizes, cups and titles, deserved or undeserved.

LISTENING TO THE WIRELESS was to undergo a complete change around 1952. The development was the arrival of Radio Luxembourg on 208 metres, and its advent was a benchmark in popular music, providing undreamt of competition for Radio Éireann. Radio Luxembourg was a commercial station which could be received all over Ireland, and it was the kiss of life to popular song-writing and performing. In November of that year the charts were invented, compiled on the sales of records for the week, and the 'Top Twenty' on Radio Luxembourg came into being. Sheet music had been the medium for popular music, right from the days when the hits had been played on battered pianos along the front at seaside resorts. Now, with improved recording processes and the invention of the extended play and long playing records, we could buy much better records. The Top Twenty lit up everyone's life. Serious and habitually grumpy people were heard to go around humming 'How Much is that Doggie in the Window?' or 'Don't let the Stars get in your Eyes'. Jo Stafford's

'You Belong to Me' and Kay Starr's 'Comes Along a Love' were sounding out night and day, and 'She Wears Red Feathers and a Hula-Hula Skirt' was a knockout altogether, with people swinging their hips as they sang it.

Romance was in for a great lift and people sang meaningful lines to each other. Most of the words of the songs seemed written specially for romantic situations, and those temporarily on the scrap heap of romance never knew whether they were going to cheer up or burst out crying at a song. The real heart-render was the Eddie Calvert Trumpet version of 'O Mein Papa', and Mantovani and his Orchestra playing 'Moulin Rouge' was sophisticated listening. This new 'pop' culture was to take strong root everywhere and it folded in nicely with all the other streams of culture flowing around us. We played the new records on a pick-up through the wireless and everyone gave parties. People's mothers tended to get the words of the new songs wrong and ours went about the house singing such incomprehensible couplets as

And the little old mill went round and round,
And so did the little old boy.

or *I'm looking over a field of clover...* instead of *four-leaved clover*, and a new release of an old song:

Let him go, let him tarry,
Let him sink or let him swim,
I'm going to marry
A far nicer him.

Vera Lynn sang 'The Homing Waltz' and Al Martino sang 'Here in my Heart' and a whole new industry came into being.

THE NEAREST THEATRE to us in Blackrock was the Globe Theatre in Dún Laoghaire. It was housed in the Gas Company and the theatre was built over the showrooms and was reached by a stairway which ran up the side of the display area. Patrons arrived deliberately early for the shows so that they

81

could inspect the latest appliances at leisure, and the 'New World' and 'Regulo' cookers were all the go. At the interval in the play, coffee and biscuits were served and the patrons would rove among the cookers, cup in hand, examining the innovations on the stoves such as pilot lights and racks for heating plates. They often got so deeply into reading advertising material that they heard the summoning bell with surprise and then remembered what had brought them to Dún Laoghaire in the first place.

The Globe presented great theatre. It was founded by Norman Rodway, Genevieve Lyons, Godfrey Quigley and Pauline Delaney, and Milo O'Shea and Maureen Toal were in many of the performances. We went to *I am a Camera* and encountered real sophistication with Genevieve Lyons in the role of Sally Bowles, black velvet beret on the side of her blonde head, long, long cigarette holder and black sequined dress, as she switched from one mood to another in a rôle that could have been written for her. *The House of Bernarda Alba* and other exciting theatre pieces from the continent curdled our blood and we hardly ever missed a show in the Gas Company, as this was international theatre on our doorstep. We were taught to recognise actors and playwrights and I remember my mother pointing out Lennox Robinson to me at a bus stop on Lansdowne Road, where he was standing holding a bunch of wild flowers. When we went to shows in town we were often brought to the stage door and we met F.J. McCormack at the Abbey and Hilton Edwards and Mícheál MacLiammóir at the Gate. I also remember seeing Jimmy O'Dea in the green room of the Gaiety talking to my father, and wondering what a 'jar' was. *Dublin Opinion* had a theatre page and tickets for first nights came into the office all the time, so there was ample opportunity for going to the theatre down the years.

The first film to send me over the moon was not any of the children's films. It was *The Tales of Hoffman* and I went into shock at the beautiful music, the scenes in the caves and the doll which had to be wound up to sing. I had never seen such combinations of beauty before and it brought me on to a whole new level of experience. As a family we did not often go to the pictures but when there was something special showing in the Regent or Tunnel in Blackrock, we would all go down to see it. Films like *The Card*, *The Ladykillers*, *Bicycle Thieves*, *Never Take No for an Answer* and *The Red Balloon* packed the Tunnel to capacity, and when the lights went up at the end of the show neighbours and acquaintances sat smiling self-consciously at one another.

7

Religion

BLACKROCK CHURCH was the centre of our spirituality. It was immensely lofty and of a frustrating design because when it had been extended to accommodate the growing population of Blackrock, the architect had merely added a second nave alongside the existing one. The effect of this was to cut the church in two so that from the side aisle there was no way in which the congregation could see the main altar. Mass was said in Latin and, as amplification had not yet been introduced, it was a touch and go business whether you heard anything the priest said. The Mass was followed in a missal and if you sat at the edge of a bench at St Anne's aisle you might catch a glimpse of the priest's chasuble swinging about and feel a little bit more in on things.

The church was further divided crossways. This was done for the purpose of money collections so that the 'poor' people could be cut off from the 'others', and the collection plates were expected to reflect the difference between the two groups. A fleet of little men with expensively-acquired purple complexions and slicked-back white hair marshalled the collection plates and, dressed in a little brief authority, their word was law. They would lock the little wooden gates between the two sections of the church before they began collecting just to be sure of the collection levels. My father greatly disapproved of such selective collecting and one Sunday morning when he came back from receiving Communion, he found the little gate locked and access to his seat barred as he had knelt behind the dividing line. He took out his silver pipe cleaner and picked the lock with one or two turns of it, found his place and went on with his thanksgiving. The collectors were aghast, for never in all their tenure had they been challenged in such a manner. The following Sunday the little gates lay open and within a short time they disappeared forever.

The great majority of people went to early Mass. Late Masses were for the very old, the convalescent and the sloppy brigade. Everyone dressed formally and we would have been very taken aback had anyone come in sweater or casual wear. It was also taken for granted that churches were cold and you just had to put on extra clothes when you were going there. Covered heads were the rule for women and they went to any lengths to hide their offending crown, so it was not unusual to see a woman coming back from the altar balancing a glove on her head, with a most devout face under it. A 'daily communicant' was a term of the deepest admiration, people blessed themselves passing every Catholic church, stopped in the street to say the Angelus and always carried a rosary beads in their pocket or handbag.

WE LOVED OUR religion. It was our mainstay and our peace of mind and it was always comfortingly there. Some of the priests might have had funny ways but these were regarded as part of the ordination package, and to be anti-clerical was to act in bad taste. The priests lived in a huge gloomy house in the church grounds and parishioners preferred to knock at the door of the brightly-lit sacristy and have their chats there instead, as the priests were very much a part of the community. Altar boys were plentiful and the church was always full to bursting point for Mass and for evening Benediction. Slipping into the church to say a prayer was routine for most people, and women always ended their shopping by popping in. I sometimes heard my mother say regretfully at the end of the day, 'Just imagine, I wasn't in a church today'.

The perpetual novena to Our Lady was held every Monday night. It was a great source of hope and confidence and if you had an intention you really wanted to obtain you attended for nine consecutive Mondays. This meant that you were transferring the responsibility for your undertaking, or request, to a more powerful and reliable authority than yourself and you were released from strain immediately. The deeper your faith, the greater your release, and we just got on with our lives in deep faith and hoped for the best, safe in the knowledge that things would work out for the best. They did too, with the odd miracle being granted and we would not have missed the novena for anything. The booming organ, the pockets of sparkling light from the flickering candles, the sweet prayers of intercession and the avowals of faith rising from the devout upturned faces spread a deep tranquillity throughout the church. The walk home after a convivial chat with neighbours also contributed to the feeling of well-being. My father came down to the novena and always enjoyed the hymn-singing and he would open up in his trained baritone voice with great gusto. 'Hail Queen of Heaven' was the closing hymn each time and he would give it his all. One night his mind was elsewhere and he ran out of words after the first line, but not a man to be daunted by anything as trivial as a lapse of memory he sang on, using 'Da Da Diddly-Um Da' as filler material. My mother brought him back to earth with a quick poke in the side.

Children's confessions were held before lunchtime on Saturdays and we went down week in, week out, rain or shine, to be shriven. Our sins were roughly the same each time but we enjoyed the absolution and would feel a glow of spiritual security coming out of the confession box. We would fling ourselves on our knees immediately to say whatever penance we had been given as part of the sacrament, as we believed a poor future awaited us in the next world if something were to happen to us on the way home and we were to pass into the next

86

world without having fulfilled our obligation. Slightly light-headed in our new-found virtue we would do figure-eights on bicycles around the church car park and then race off home to Saturday dinner of boiled ham and parsley sauce. I forgot my beret one Saturday and put on a white rubber bathing hat as head covering before sailing into the box quite unaware of the effect. The priest gave a huge start and then recovered himself sufficiently to hear my sins. On my way out he said kindly that he hoped I would be well soon again and I thanked him timidly and left the box thinking I had committed a minor sin by not telling him my head was normal, and then I left it to God to sort the thing out.

I LIKED TO WATCH the banks of lighted candles on the stands during Mass and to frighten myself by calling each after different people and then watching to see which one burnt down the quickest. Some would burn fiercely and others would just flicker, depending on the draughts in the church and I would feel sad for a few moments about the person who had been extinguished first. It was always a relief when I went first as I didn't have to feel guilty about anyone else. Since I often could not see what was going on at the main altar and some of the priests took a long time over Mass, this exercise was a reserve tank against fidgeting.

There was a very holy man called Mr Dowling who used to pray in front of the altar with his head on one side and his hands clasped tightly. Levitation had been explained to us in school as part of the lives of some saints and we used to check on Mr Dowling frequently in case he took off when we weren't looking. Families knelt in rows and filed up to Communion sedately, so that if there was any reason why you should not receive, this would have caused you great difficulty. I once went through a frightful crisis when, on the way out to Mass, I ate a knob of icing from a cake which had been left out after a party the night before; I just popped it in going by. The fast from midnight was kept rigidly at the time and some people didn't even wash their teeth in case they swallowed water and broke their fast, so I was horrified when, just as I was going up to the altar, I remembered the ingestion of the offending item of tuck. I couldn't drop out of the line and so I went up with everyone else and practically fainted on the way down, thinking I had received unworthily. I had to wait a whole deathly week until Saturday confession by which time I was virtually in a decline, as I thought the matter too serious to discuss with anyone but the priest. To my surprise the priest was very nice about it, and in the end I felt slightly let down as I had expected a massive penance. We were well coached in penance and I thought this might be my big moment for breaking into the next round of sanctity.

We were extremely fond of doing penance for the Holy Souls in Purgatory. We heard a lot about them in school and were very much on their side. There was also the hope that they would do the necessary for us when they were safe in Heaven and we might be in a spot of trouble ourselves. Going to school on bitterly cold mornings we would remove our gloves and march along stoically with blue outstretched fingers, or cycle with our hands freezing on the handlebars and offer up the pain for the Holy Souls. For the same purpose we often put pebbles in our shoes and piously hobbled along for three or four lamp posts or until we could go no further. All this effort brought us great satisfaction and that bit nearer to the child saints of whom we had heard so much in *The Imeldist* magazine, which recounted heroic deeds done by teenies. We calculated how much the Holy Souls were getting out of our supportive efforts and when one of the family was reproved by my mother for eating sweets during Lent she gravely replied: 'You may not know it but I am expecting two Holy Souls out of Purgatory next Tuesday'. Lent came and went each year with various efforts at self-denial. We gave up sweets immediately each time but very few stayed the course. We would buy them and put them in jam jars and gaze at them until eventually the flesh weakened. My brother even gave up beetroot for Lent, as he liked the bottled variety so much. It was a reasonable assumption that he would not have to face too much temptation at that time of year as salad time had not yet arrived.

I HAD A GREAT religious secret to keep. We had heard much about visions and I was deeply impressed by them. I had been told that Jesus lived in the tabernacle and I resolved that I would try and get a look at him when the priest opened the little door to put back the communion vessels. Everyone would be in a head-down position saying their thanksgiving and if I stood up quickly and then sat down I might manage it undetected. I waited and watched for my opportunity and on the following Sunday I got it. The family knelt near the front of the church and I took up a position at the end of the bench to cut down disturbance of next of kin; when the priest opened the doors I shot up over the sea of heads, the little doors swung back and I saw it all – the Lord, sufficiently small in stature to fit in the tabernacle – reclining on a couch on one elbow, looking out pleasantly in my direction. I was absolutely thrilled and sank back secure in the knowledge that I too had had a vision and was on course for being a child saint. I did not reveal this exquisite secret to anyone and it was not too many years later that it dawned on me that I just might not have had a vision after all.

PROCESSIONS WERE BIG at the time. The May procession and the Corpus Christi procession were large-scale undertakings with everyone dressed in white and a route which led to the private part of the school grounds, the cloister gardens. Satin banners with extracts from prayers fluttered in the breeze and hymns wafted back half a tone lower in pitch as we wound around corners. We loved it all, the rose petals scattered on the route and the whole ceremonial aspect and attention to detail. One year during the procession I was greatly distracted. I saw many sturdy feathers along the route dropped by large birds and left ungathered and I thought of my father's antique brass quill maker. I could have a whole new collection of pens if I gathered up the feathers as we wound our way along, and so I darted in and out of line, piously joining in every refrain and hymn while I harvested this treasure trove. I stuffed them down the front of my white dress but alas, my unusual shape for a juvenile was noticed and they were all taken away from me and I was severely rebuked. I could never quite work out what was irreverent and what was not.

May altars went up every year with our large statue of Our Lady flanked by vases of garden flowers. One year we got tiny statues from Lourdes and we put up miniature altars all over the house with forget-me-nots in thimbles each side of them and we thought they were just lovely. There was an all-time low one night when my brothers were in giddy mood and began to skim their school caps around their bedroom. The May altar was in one corner and they whirled the caps around, never thinking they would hit the statue, but to their horror the large statue got clipped by the cap and it fell on the vases, bringing the whole altar down in a mess of shards, broken vases, water and flowers. Their contrition was deep but their faith must have been even deeper, because when my mother was going by their room later on, she heard them praying, 'Oh Jesus, put the bits together, Oh Jesus, put the bits together'.

Scapulars were very popular as were medals worn on chains and everyone wore a Miraculous medal. It was not unusual for people to wear several medals around their neck and to rattle around with a fair amount of metal on them. We were encouraged to put the scapulars between our mattresses rather than around our necks, as they had to be washed too frequently and wore out as a result.

VISITING SEVEN CHURCHES was a penitential exercise set for Holy Thursday. The altars arranged for exposition of the Blessed Sacrament were exquisitely decorated with flowers and candles and we thoroughly enjoyed this so-called penance, tearing from church to church on bicycles and comparing notes with friends as to how many they had visited and which was the most beautiful. It was our chance to break the fastnesses of religious institutions such as the Vincentians and the French Sisters of Charity on the Back Road and all the convents around. We thought the French Sisters were very impressive with their white birds'-wings headdresses, and one year my father put them on the *Dublin Opinion* Christmas card. We liked the Carmelite Convent in Sweetman's Avenue in Blackrock and got to know the sacristan, Mother Thérèse, very well. She trained my brothers as altar boys and they enjoyed going there as she always invited them to breakfast after Mass and treated them like the priests. She would chat to them through the black curtain and inadvertently make them laugh when she said things like, 'Enjoy those eggs, now boys, they're our own'. I was in on some of these visits and naturally the strict enclosure of the Carmelites was a source of fascination to us as we had never seen Mother Thérèse without the curtain. One day we vowed to break her enclosure and when she arranged to leave some brown bread in the porch for us we rushed her, flinging open the door and smiling cheerily into her horrified face.

Early on she asked me whether I would like to become a Carmelite and she gave me the autobiography of Saint Teresa to read. I enjoyed it very much and considered the proposition well, but I made sure to tell her that first I would have to travel all over the world and see rather a lot of it. Mother Thérèse must have decided that maybe I was poor Carmelite material after all.

THE INFINITE HELD FEAR for me and the term 'for ever and ever' was something with which I could not come to terms. I hoped that if I went to Heaven a special arrangement might be made for me so that I wouldn't be aware that this new life would go on and on. Maybe God would arrange for me to go to sleep, so that I wouldn't notice. This seemed an ungrateful thought but I firmly decided to talk the matter out on arrival so that my pleasure would not be marred in any way. Infinity reared its ugly head in small ways. One was the tin of Royal Baking Powder. The tin was decorated with an oval which contained an exact replica of the tin itself complete with lettering. This tin, in turn, had its tin with a little oval inside it and so on and I used to open the kitchen press and take it out and stare at it until I felt queasy and then put it swiftly back again.

There was an allegorical picture in the music room of the

91

junior school which depicted Saint Joseph offering the child Jesus a large platter of fruit. Holy pictures were inclined to feature unlikely scenes from the Gospels and this one was happily accepted by me as 'the fruit of thy womb, Jesus'. Religious terms were often left unexplained and in some cases we just settled for whatever meaning we gave the words ourselves. The Maynooth catechism was our staple diet and we sometimes gave answers to complicated questions without being at all clear, using such words as 'consanguinity', with only the dimmest idea of what it was all about.

THE ROSARY WAS RECITED widely and the family rosary was given out in nearly every home, ours being no exception. It was generally much loved as a prayer, being revered as the means by which Ireland had kept the Faith in times of religious persecution. My father always lead the rosary, starting its recitation with a Creed, three Hail Marys and a Glory-be before settling down to the first decade. He would then call on others to take the following decades and we had to pay attention. One sister was absent-minded and always forgot her beads, another mumbled her decade into the seat of her armchair and we never knew when she had finished it, one brother took ages over his and I said either one Hail Mary too many or too few. The two other brothers had to pray at opposite ends of the room to avoid the onset of jellified giggles. The budgie had a habit of ringing his bell at the end of a decade when the voices dropped and this used to reduce them to a pitiable state, but my mother who had long experience of quelling gigglers, would merely give them a long questioning look, which was usually sufficient to restore decorum.

The rosary constituted a real dilemma for us as regards getting our homework done. It was said nightly around the study fire some time between tea and supper and the dilemma for us lay not so much in the recital of the prayer, but in the fact that the fire-huggers downstairs had the power to set the time for it, rather than those of us doing our homework in various rooms about the house. When concentration had at last been garnered and the homework was going well, the cry of 'rosary' would ring throughout the house and once you left your books and the spartan conditions of the bedroom to join the jolly warmth of the study, it was nearly impossible to return. When we heard the familiar muezzin's cry we would groan in despair of ever getting the load of work shifted, throw down our pens and go down reluctantly to where luckier people were reading, gossiping or listening to the radio.

After years of such summonses my sister and I finally reached such a point of exasperation in the face of Christmas tests that we decided to take action. One night we piously said our rosary together and then got down to homework. The familiar cry came from the hall and we didn't answer. After repeating the call, a messenger came up to know what was happening and we sent down a dignified message that we had said ours and would not be coming down. An interval passed, the door opened and my father came in and looked at us gravely, eliciting an explanation. We explained our position and he just gave us a long hard look and left, presuming that we would return shortly to the fold, but we never did when we had homework to do.

A milestone was the Confirmation pledge when we promised not to take any alcoholic drink until we were twenty-one. It never occurred to any of us to break it and at ten years of age one of my brothers even asked my mother for a glass of sherry on the night before his Confirmation, so that he could remember the sensation and taste and know what he was giving up.

A REALLY NICE PROTESTANT lady called Mrs Fry lived near the end of Avoca Avenue and she met one of my brothers in the local shop and kindly bought him a large ice-cream. He was still quite small so my mother was quite mystified when he told her, 'Naturally I pretended to eat it but threw it in the hedge when we got past her gate and I was on my own again'. When my mother enquired, 'Whatever for?' he said in a reproachful voice, 'It might have been poisoned', and my mother had a vision of charming Mrs Fry secretly signalling to the shop assistant to take out the ice-cream block marked 'poison' to serve her young neighbour.

All in all, Protestants continued to fascinate us. A phrase much in use at the time was 'They're Protestants but they're very nice'. This was said with an air of gentle tolerance. 'You're a proper little Protestant' was not an unusual form of address by a young mother to her baby if it had to be taken out of the church at Mass time for crying.

Some Catholics vaguely thought that Protestants were English. There was little relationship between the two main denominations and quite a lot of confusion. The tangible differences were that nearly all Protestants seemed to have telephones, refrigerators and cars, and they tilled their gardens and grew their own vegetables. They mainly drove Austin, Morris, Standard or Hillman cars. Catholics, on the other hand, were more likely to have Fords, Volkswagens or Fiats and were slower to acquire modern conveniences such as refrigerators.

Protestants lived in a world of their own and we believed everything we were told about them by other children. A boy living near us went to school in Dún Laoghaire and had to pass 'The Birds' Nest', a Protestant orphanage. He and his friends used to run past the high granite building in York Road until they were clear of it, firmly believing that if they walked by they could be grabbed in and reared as Protestants. They would never see their parents again and, worse still, they would have to become Protestants.

Protestant children were immediately recognisable and they also knew us on sight. In summer we spotted them by their nice tanned legs. I don't know why Protestant skin was always, or nearly always, a nice olive brown, but brown legs they had, to our everlasting envy. Protestant girls were allowed to wear ankle socks out of season and we called their legs 'Protestant brown', whereas we were ignominiously put into long lisle stockings on the first day back in September. The Protestant boys were mostly very handsome and they rode by to Avoca school with their hockey sticks across their handlebars, with straight blond hair and haughty faces. We admired them extravagantly and even when a Protestant school, St

Andrew's, was beaten ninety-seven duck in school's rugby and made history thereby, we still thought Protestant boys were most attractive. The Hall School girls were cause for bated breath, with blond shiny hair and dressed in green and grey, with immensely short skirts. Catholic boys had never seen anything so beautiful and we were totally diminished in our long navy gymslips. These girls would call loudly to one another on the tops of buses and they had funny names as if they had been christened out of schoolgirl stories, such as Bunny, Tuffy and Bunty, with some called Wendy, Cheryl or Sue.

We took pride in the fact that our neighbours on both sides were Protestant as we had moved into a new district by moving to Avoca Avenue. One set gave tennis parties and wore floppy colonial hats while playing. Tea would be rolled out on a trolley by Molly the maid and this family and their guests would play tennis late into the summer evenings. They also had a gardener who came every day and produced fruit and vegetables for the table.

The neighbours on the other side were strictly anti-social and the elderly Protestant lady disliked us so much that when we were out snowballing she would walk by several times in the hope of being hit. They were a mother and son and, as we never saw anyone enter their home, we wondered how two people could rattle around so much in all that space. They used to do a great deal of clanking of buckets and sometimes we joked that they were feeding imaginary farm animals. The son was a grown man, handsome and moody-looking, and we called him Oily Ollie on account of his olive brown complexion and Brylcreamed hair. He held great allure for us in that we had been told that he had studied for Holy Orders, but had stopped short of ordination by fainting out cold at the moment of taking his final vow. We liked to imagine the scene and describe it to one another, conjuring up the deathly pallor of his handsome countenance, the sudden swoon, the recoiling in horror of the congregation and the slow darkening of the church over the scene. We watched him go shopping gloomily on his bicycle, a leather shopping bag on the handlebars, and he eventually broke his own spell by unexpectedly getting off his bicycle one day and blocking my sister's way on the path, staring at her and telling her that she would be very good-looking when she grew up.

As well as Protestant brown there was a colour called 'Protestant grey'. This was the dark grey colour favoured by the old ladies of Glenageary who dressed in it from top to toe ending with high-heeled grey leather one-button-and-strap shoes. We couldn't imagine them dressing otherwise and they could never, ever, even in a fit of madness, have worn red or any primary colour. The heavier of the Protestant ladies had bandaged legs, presumably for varicose veins and we considered this rather Protestant too. The Glenageary and Glasthule ladies also had slanted eyelids, and this type of physiognomy was referred to as the 'Glenageary slant'. The Protestants at Seapoint and Killiney beach were easily marked out by their natty swimwear. Catholics just didn't seem to achieve this style with their 'bathing costumes' or 'togs' and we envied the Jansen swimwear of the Protestants, with the little diver on the hip.

There was a Presbyterian church near our home and we liked to watch the congregation gather for Evensong. Old editions of good cars would roll up and sensibly-dressed people, few in number compared to our teeming hordes, would descend and walk stiffly to the church door where the minister would be waiting to greet them. This could never have happened in our churches with their thousands of worshippers converging on the church at the same time. We were most interested in the two kinds of worship and as children we felt really sorry for those Protestants, going to all that trouble to pray when they were on what we regarded as the wrong road.

We had a secret which we found quite hard to keep. Each year when we went on holidays to County Wicklow we would pay a visit to the Protestant church at Preban on Sunday afternoon when there was no one about. We would steal in and do something which we regarded as rather frightful, and that was to read the Bible. We would stand on tiptoe in front of the great book on its brass eagle stand and read out a few words in a sepulchral voice, and then wait to see in what way God's anger would be visited upon us. Reading the Bible was not allowed to us so we were trespassing spiritually as well as materially. After a few runs at it we would lose our nerve and sneak out hurriedly, sometimes genuflecting in confusion.

When one of our Wicklow Protestant friends died, our parents brought us to the funeral, although such attendances were not permitted. We did not dream of entering the church during the service but took our places by the open grave with a sense of adventure. We felt so sad for Ned Boyd, for he had been such a nice man and now he was dead and had no further chance of becoming a Catholic.

8

Food

CATERING IN MY MOTHER'S generation revolved around
bread and meat. This is not to say that there was any scarcity
of milk or vegetables, butter, jam or other commodities, but
the heart and core of catering for a large family lay in an abundant supply of meat and the staff of life. Occasionally a des-
pairing cry would ring through the house, 'There's no bread'.

'No bread?'

'No bread.'

My mother would be panic-stricken and all activity would
be halted as in the presence of some great calamity.

'How could there possibly be no bread?' my mother
would ask as if betrayed. 'I must get to the bottom of this'.
And so the investigation would be undertaken and the offend-
er or eater of the last slice of bread would be dispatched to
Blackrock on a bicycle, no matter how late the hour, to find a
shop which still had bread for sale. Bread was sometimes
made at home too, either by my mother or the current maid.
Usually it came to the side door in the baker's basket and featured mainly loaves and turnovers which were delicious when
fresh, but rapidly turned stodgy and had to be eaten up just

the same. Anyone starting a fresh loaf while there was still some stodgy stuff in the bread bin would have to answer up and sometimes it was hard to keep ahead of the stodge.

Meat was the second master in the quartermaster's store and like everyone else we had a large roast for Sunday lunch, all the year round. There was no question of skipping the Sunday lunch and having the dinner in the evening instead. Such frivolous thinking would not get far. Sunday lunch was served at half-past one, in fact not long after a large fried breakfast had been consumed. The breakfast on a Sunday always followed eight o'clock Mass and it was a lovely crispy interesting fry together with plates of fried bread and pots of tea, a fire going early and Sunday papers to accompany it. Therefore, it was always with dismay that the smell of meat beginning to roast reached me, as the large leg of lamb or round of beef began 'to take' in the oven. I could happily have drifted on all day until evening showing no interest in food, but we were in the roast beef brigade and there was no escaping it. Until Sunday lunch was tackled and eaten no other activity was contemplated. To top the matter my father and brothers would never come down to eat it on time as they always wanted to finish listening to 'The Billy Cotton Band Show' on BBC radio. Nobody would ever have suggested listening to the radio while eating, or moving the wireless from the study to the dining-room, as temporary arrangements were unthinkable and anyway the wireless weighed a ton. When lunch was over we would stream away to our separate lives and come back in stages, as Sunday tea was an unstructured affair, often served from a trolley beside the study fire and consisting of ham sandwiches, pancakes or drop scones and maybe a homemade sponge cake or two.

The ham dominated the weekend. Every Saturday a nine-pounder was cooked, as my mother had great faith in ham as a stand-by. It would appear in all forms, as the main course on Saturday, in salads, in late-night suppers, as sandwiches. It would simmer on the Aga for hours on end. Our friends would come into the house over the weekend and ask 'Where's the ham?' and then we would go down and cut what we wanted from it. One night very late, my mother heard noises and came down to investigate. She found a friend of my brother's standing on the table with the ham held aloft on a carving fork, slicing pieces off it for a hungry crowd. She gave a gracious bow and withdrew to a chorus of 'Compliments to the cook'.

WE MADE FUDGE and toffee frequently. Old saucepans were used and we eventually made fudge quite well, preferring it to toffee which was liable to burn. We never seemed to make enough of it, as once the word went out people would gather softly and mysteriously, and we could disregard the last part of the recipe which ran: 'Cut the fudge carefully in squares and store between layers of grease-proof paper in a cool dry place until required'.

We did not eat as much in the way of sweets as other children, chiefly because pocket money was in shorter supply. However, when funds allowed, the favourites were acid drops, bullseyes, Peggy's leg, liquorice in the form of pipes, strings and allsorts, conversation lozenges with illegible messages on them, and fizzbags if your family allowed them to be bought. Clove rock was popular, as were Cleeve's toffees in the large squares and there was a yellow toffee sold by Noblett's in town at their corner sweetshops near the Gaiety Theatre and in Dawson Street. Peppermint creams, fudge and Scots Clan toffees were in the next round as they were sold by the quarter, as were Lemon's pure sweets, which meant that there had to be a back-up of money somewhere. Coughnomore was a liquorice toffee which nearly pulled the teeth from the gums but was very good for lasting on the train all the way home from music lessons. Frys' Crunchies were beloved and the range of chocolate bars was between Cadbury's and Rowntree's, with Cadbury's the runaway leader.

My father loved coffee and drank a large pot of it every morning. The first sip and savour was always a little ceremony and he would pronounce on the flavour with great gravity. He would often arrive home with a new percolator, a miracle coffee bean grinder, a newly-featured jug and strainer by

Bewley's or a new blend of coffee, fully expecting everyone to be as excited about it as he was, although he would probably be the only one to benefit from it.

POPULAR FAMILY FOOD was shepherd's pie, fish pie, corned beef and cabbage, brown stew or Irish stew, and steak and kidney pie.

Since meat was plentiful and inexpensive, soup was always meat-based and bowls of chicken or mutton broth were usual occupants of the green wooden safe which stood in the yard outside the kitchen. Chickens were simmered as 'in case' food and this meant plenty of chicken broth. Whenever my mother bought minced meat she bought steak in the butcher's, had the butcher clean out the mincer before her eyes and then mince her particular piece. In this way she was sure that no inferior meat might get mixed up with hers and she would get her full weight of prime steak freshly minced. My father liked kippers occasionally but we children were not very impressed with them.

One meal we absolutely loved was rabbit pie. The rabbits were wild and gamey and my mother would cook them slowly in the Aga and then cover the big casserole with pastry half dipping into the rich gravy. The aroma of this coming out of the Aga, just cooked, was enough to bring tears to your eyes on a cold day. Mid-week, when we came home late from the piano lessons in the Academy she often had beef kidney chopped up small in its own delicious gravy hemmed in by a ring of creamed potatoes. We thought that this was one of the loveliest meals in the world, but my pure delight was chicken broth and this was often on the go, particularly if someone in the house was unwell. My mother's chicken broth, with a touch of onion and all the grease removed, would have put life into a statue.

PASTRY WAS MUCH in evidence, coming to the fore in apple tarts, fish pie or pastry sticks. Making it was not thought labour intensive and it was drummed up at the drop of a hat to extend dishes and fill up the family. It appeared again in the guise of apple dumplings which my father liked extravagantly and which we all hated. Apple Charlotte, apple sponge and apple everything else were regulars, bread and butter pudding was made when too much leftover bread had backed up and we went through the normal range of milk puddings with the exception of tapioca because of its similarity to frogspawn. A pudding to which I was personally addicted was junket, made by adding rennet to milk. I used to volunteer to make it at weekends and I would delight in making large bowls of this kind of pudding for family consumption. Carageen moss jelly was a doubtful runner up in the popularity stakes and something called 'jelly-fuzz', a kind of soufflé made with tinned milk, was an all-time favourite.

Some 'shop' cakes were great favourites, the chocolate pipe cake from Mitchell's for one. When factory shop cakes came on the market they were received with great caution, in spite of the cheery advertising in the form of comic strips about hens laying the eggs specially for the cakes. 'Made with fresh fruit, butter and eggs', ran the slogan, but it was hard to convince the home-bakers, who were heard to tell one another that they were made with seagulls' eggs. I had a picture of men climbing up cliff faces to get the eggs at the peril of their lives and thought it rather sad that all this effort was dismissed so lightly.

AFTERNOON TEA was the daytime social occasion among married women and my mother often held one. The preparations would start two days beforehand with a great cleaning down of the house and general inspection of appointments. Flowers would be bought and arranged, and a general air of casual well-being was the aim. In summer a nest of tables would be sited near an open window to enjoy a view of the garden, and in winter the afternoon tea would be positioned around a glowing fire in the drawing room. It was considered good form to wheel in a trolley-full of goodies when a dignified interval had elapsed after the arrival of the ladies and the small chat was setting up nicely. The ladies would arrive in ones and twos wearing felt hats with little veils stitched on to them, long silk gloves in summer and long leather ones in winter. My mother once complimented one of her afternoon tea friends on the variety of hats, and received the reply, 'You can't disappoint people, Kathleen'.

These were well-covered ladies wearing silky, flowery cross-over dresses in warm weather and a similar style in good wool cloth in winter, topped by fur coats. Coats and gloves were removed on arrival but hats remained firmly pinned on. The ladies discussed families, schools and domestic help, with now and then an effort to tackle world affairs. They would help themselves to a large range of sandwiches, cream cakes, scones, butter, jam and other dainties, which helped to explain why they all thought they might be carrying a little too much weight. Hot apple tart topped with whipped cream was the litmus test of a good afternoon tea and the time would pass pleasantly enough until about five-thirty, when they would all realise that it was indeed time to go home to tea.

A continental family lived near us and my mother was often asked to their home for afternoon tea; indeed this happened so frequently that she decided that she must constitute a good example of native culture. Baronesses and countesses would gather and the conversation would range over a much wider set of subjects than at native afternoon teas. The continental ladies had plaited coils of hair and crested rings and were mostly the wives of men in the diplomatic corps. The cakes were always well above the Irish ones, with a long tradition of confectionery behind them. Strudel with creamy wine sauce was one of their delicacies. The hostess could never understand how Irish people balanced cups of tea, plates of sandwiches and dainties, and still managed to eat elegantly. She would sit her guests down to a sensible table and serve coffee in tiny shell-like cups and encourage the guests to work their way through a tremendous spread. My mother used to ask the continental lady back on a one-to-three basis and thoroughly enjoyed these trips into European society.

9

Consumer Goods

SMOKING WAS PART of living. It was expected that adults would smoke and every provision was made so that they did so in comfort. Christmas presents generally nurtured the habit of smoking and tin boxes of Capstan Mild, Players Navy Cut, Craven A and other brands were popular. Overseas brands in evidence were State Express and Star and American brands such as Philip Morris and Marlborough were regarded as style. Smokers could be sure of getting at least 200 cigarettes in a decorative box at Christmas to keep them calm in the days or weeks to come. Cut glass ashtrays were top of the special presents and cigarette caskets and table lighters were big. Top of the range lighters had classical designs and the middle of the range of cigarette boxes played 'Arivederci Roma' when you opened them. Cigarette cases were plated and solid silver with initials and were often matched with lighters and there was even one super-duper one which had a lighter built into the side of it, with which men used to cut a dash at dress dances. Girls were given a Dunhill lighter when things were looking good with the boyfriend, the first pledge towards the gold bracelet, the watch and eventually the ring.

Most working men smoked and they often had a cigarette behind their ear. The brand for the plain working man was 'Woodbine', a cheap cigarette sold singly and in packets and it was not uncommon to see a man take a burnt cigarette butt from behind his ear and resume an interrupted smoke.

Health did not come into this at all, although there was still much tuberculosis about. Cigarette advertisements bore no health warnings, in fact they personalised and idealised the smoking habit as the ideal for the well-adjusted person, and featured high-profile society figures bent on enjoying their cigarette.

Non-smokers were the exception. The upper decks of buses were caverns of smoke when they were full, and on a winter's evening it was a choice between dying of suffocation or opening the window and getting a blast of cold wind in your eye all the way home. Clothes often smelt of smoke, and coughing and throat-clearing were the norm. Although 'spitting forbidden' notices had gone out with the trams, they were still needed to some extent. The trip on the morning bus was a cacophony of throat clearing and the church was not much better.

Fingers ranged in colour from palest lemon to darkest burnt-orange and it was quite normal and acceptable to have nicotine stains on hands and nails, particularly for men. Even for women diamond rings and nicotine stains were not mutually exclusive. My father smoked a pipe as did just about everyone's father and he kept his tobacco in a blue and brown tobacco jar with a tightly closed lid. Pipes were noisy things with much scratching and scraping of the bowl between smokes, and men whacked their pipes off their shoes to get the last bit of burnt-out matter before starting up a new smoke, with much sucking in of air and poop-poop noises until a glow to their liking had been established. Most tobaccos smelt nicely, but some were rather awful and you could be properly trapped if a pipe smoker sat down at your table in a restaurant and you didn't care for his tobacco. Advertisements for tobacco celebrated manly pipe-smokers, and knitting patterns invariably had a man smoking a pipe when illustrating jumpers

105

and pullovers. In some rural areas the white clay dúidín was still smoked, sometimes with the stem burnt away. I once found an old pipe in a stable when we were down in the country on holidays and delighted its owner by returning it to him. It just looked like a dirty old pipe to me.

ADVERTISING WAS in its infancy. The first electric sign in Dublin was the Bovril sign, done in bulbs and positioned over Fox's cigar merchants at O'Connell Bridge. The lights fanned up in various colours behind the bottle and everyone loved it. The Donnelly's sausage sign was probably Dublin's first neon sign, and it was also cause for excitement. The name Donnelly had been split into two names, Don and Nelly and these exciting and original characters tossed a skinless sausage back and forth between two frying pans. We thought we were in New York every time we saw it and we used to sing the jingle from the sponsored radio programme with great energy:

> So the next time you go to your grocers,
> Tell him no other sausage will do.
> To all his suggestions say 'No, Sir'.
> It's Donnelly's, Donnelly's for you.

Another advertisement which ruled the waves was the one which told you that McBirney's was 'Forty paces from O'Connell Bridge'. This was beaten home so often in their advertising that one day when I was in town to get buttons in Trimmings on the quays I got off the bus and measured the paces seriously for myself. I got forty-two paces instead of forty and I seriously considered writing to McBirney's to tell them about their miscalculation and encourage them to change their advertising.

The Imco cleaning and dyeing company also had a sponsored programme and its jingle was of the order of:

> They do get weary,
> Women do get weary,
> Wearing the same shabby dress.
> And when they're weary,
> Try an Imco dye and press!

THE IRISH HOSPITALS' TRUST was part of the lifestream of the country. It was the gambling backdrop in the absence of a national lottery and people bought tickets for £1, ten shillings for a half share and five shillings for a quarter share. Almost invariably the winners seemed to come from the United States and Canada. We knew a family in Monkstown who once won the sweep and every time the draw came round my parents forgot to buy tickets and then bemoaned the fact that they never won anything. Each time there was a prominent horse race, a monster draw for horses was held at the premises of the Hospitals' Trust in Ballsbridge. Pretty nurses would line up beside a large drum and pull the tickets out of portholes, and huge prizes would be won on the results of the race some days afterwards. You could visit the Sweep and see the drum which caused all the excitement, but when I saw it I thought it looked very dull, rather like an old boiler.

The Irish Hospitals' Sweepstake sponsored radio programme came out every night at ten o'clock and it was my curfew call as I was expected to be home by ten. I would rise in panic in friends' houses if I heard the signature tune, 'Makes no difference where you are, you can wish upon a star', and the fruity voice of Bart Bastable introducing the programme, and make the trip back home in record time. My mother often heard my flying feet from the top of Avoca Avenue on a summer's night as I sprinted home, rather than break the trust established about being back on time.

1948 BROUGHT AN END to the trams. There were two kinds, the ones with the open tops being the most popular with children, although it was hard to persuade adults to go up there as they were not interested in being hit in the face with rain or having their hats whirl away in the wind. The second type had closed top decks but still afforded a fine view. When the tram reached the terminus the trolley had to be reversed and small boys used to leap down and ask the driver if they could help him. A little conductor's seat was positioned behind the driver's door and this had to be carried to the other end of the tram each time it reached the end of the line. When the last tram left Nelson's Pillar for Dalkey, people tore souvenirs off it such as seats and anything else that could be removed, so that when it reached the terminus for the last time it was a shaking frame. Another phase in the life of Dublin had come to a close.

IT WAS EXCITING living near Blackrock Baths and spending every summer there. When mentioned anywhere in the country the name conjured up scenes of international swimming galas and great drama. When a gala was held the swimming lanes were marked out in the 'international' size pool by ropes and wooden balls, and divers would come to practise from the diving platform which was thirty-three feet high. Divers came from Britain and our own Eddie Heron was the Irish contender for the big titles. We used to sit in rows spellbound as they went through the numbers from their repertoire, and as there was no television then to bring us live coverage of diving or other sports, the sight was all the more spectacular. We huddled on damp benches and watched it all.

The baths were a guaranteed source of enjoyment. We were taught to swim and dive every morning and to bring up objects from the floor of the deep pool to extend our underwater endurance. Young Leinster and Sandycove Swimming Club took us as members and there was an air of glamour about the place. Sometimes we had our photograph in the paper as the baths always made news and photographers would often drop out for a story and fill up with general shots. Music was played over a loudspeaker to train swimmers in rhythmic swimming and we spent one whole summer swimming to 'Goodbye, Goodbye' from *White Horse Inn*, as they were short of gramophone records.

To be in on the full social life of the summer you had to spend the mornings in Blackrock Baths and the afternoons in Dún Laoghaire Baths, otherwise you simply did not know what was going on and acquired no social skills. The mandatory system made it possible for friendships started in one place to be developed or curtailed easily, a splendid arrangement if all was going well and a cruel one if it was not. As our parents were unlikely to finance a mass move by bus every day to the alternative spot, we either went on bicycles or stayed in Blackrock Baths and lost track of the goings on in the first league of socialising.

REGULAR VISITS to the Spring and Horse Shows were part of our growing up, and we went every year to both shows and solemnly watched demonstrations of dull household utensils and farm implements, and collected mounds of advertising material to be thrown in the bin when we got home. We always brought a picnic which we had sitting on uncomfortable rustic benches in the music tent but it was the done thing to sit there and listen to the band and we naturally conformed.

The best part of the visit to the show was the jumping. Our legs would nearly fall off from standing so long on the cement terraces with not much of a view over the high yellow hedges, and we had to leap into the air at specific points to see the action. The atmosphere was set by the muffled voice coming over the microphone announcing the names of Broom, Ringrose, Campion, Kellett and d'Annunzio, and I used to bring a box brownie to photograph the dignitaries arriving or catch an occasional photograph of a horse's tail going over a jump.

10

The War

FROM THE TIME we were old enough to have a slight grasp of what was happening in the big world outside our home, there had always been a war on. 'There's a war on', was the reply when wishes could not be fulfilled. The arrangement appeared somewhat unfair as the decisions went against us and yet the whole matter was very far away and seemed quite irrelevant to our lives. The war naturally affected supply and demand. To us it meant grey bread, grey writing paper, sandy, sickening cocoa, ration books, scratchy school jumpers and only having seen bananas and oranges pictured in books. The expression 'pre-war' connoted something wonderful, something out of reach, something of first quality. The high point for me was being brought to the town hall with the rest of the family to be fitted for a gas mask, and the big disappointment was that we never got a chance to use them. We had taken them home in high excitement but we only used them for frightening one another when we had run out of things to do on wet days. Before we put them on we chanted a ditty which ran:

Underneath the spreading chestnut tree,
De Valera said to me:
If you want to get your gas mask free,
Join the Irish A R P.

The threat of the arrival of the gas inspector or 'glimmer-man' was ever present. The glimmer was the residue of the gas supply left in the pipes when the gas was cut off because of rationing, and it was absolutely forbidden to use this for cooking. Inspectors went around on bicycles, knocking on doors at random and they were fully entitled to enter a person's home and go to their kitchen to see whether or not the cooker was being used. If they found the gas being used they cut off the supply immediately. It was a delicious bogeyman arrangement for adults, and the people who made illegal cups of tea during rationing hours on the glimmer were like those savouring a drink during prohibition. We got a primus stove run on paraffin and it involved a lot of huffing and puffing and pumping, so that it was something of a triumph when the blue flame steadied down and an extra kettle began to sing. We boiled eggs on it when we returned from early Mass on Sunday mornings.

Everything was hoarded during the war and people kept the most unlikely things 'just in case'. When we moved house we had to employ a local man with transport to come several times and remove some of the collections. He took away such items as a cobbler's last for mending shoes, some out-of-order heaters, even the ear trumpet and some odd surgical equipment which we had found in 'Rosemount' when we moved in. All this stocking and storing meant that the airing cupboard or 'hot press' was packed solid with items of clothing, and sometimes several layers of summer dresses fell on your head when you were extricating a clean pair of pyjamas. Family life went on to a background of 'The Emergency', and from time to time the voice of William Joyce came over the wireless. Once the war was ended, English people came over to Ireland in their thousands to nourish themselves and their children for the first time in years.

A HANG-OVER from the war was the allotments of land leased to members of the Mount Street Club at Booterstown marsh. Every evening they would work their squares of cabbages and onions, and self-sufficiency became fashionable with people starting to grow their own vegetables, something they could have been doing all along. This entailed a potato patch in the back garden, and some even planted potatoes in their front gardens to let the neighbours know what good citizens they were, much to the embarrassment of the children of the time. To see your lovely front lawn torn up and plebeian potatoes sown in rows was mortifying and I was heartily glad that our garden did not lend itself to such moves, as the lawn was sunken and therefore unsuitable for horticulture, though I doubt if my father would have embraced self-sufficiency. Another practice which children found witheringly embarrassing was the delivery of horse manure for the roses and fruit trees in the garden. This was before the time of commercial soil-enricher and there were no jolly bags with pictures of blooms on them, so one of the most frightful things that could happen was the arrival at your gate of a huge disgusting heap of manure to be forked into the garden by its purchaser.

In the immediate post-war years we were asked in school to bring in clothes we no longer needed so that they could be sent to Europe by the Red Cross. My mother was delighted by this forced opportunity of clearing the house, as the hoarding during the war meant that we had no space for anything new. We were sent off to school each day with large bags of castoffs which we were also delighted to get out of our lives. The Red Cross had particularly asked for underwear since bombed-out children without clothes were unlikely to be nicely kitted out with underwear, Chilprufe or otherwise. I remember when it came to my turn to empty the bag into the great basket that I nearly fainted with embarrassment as all our surplus underwear tumbled out. My friends laughed themselves silly at the volume, asking me whether we would get through the winter at all in the circumstances.

Another agonising practice was the counting of the coal

bags whenever a lorry load was delivered to the house. Our coal-house was in an enclosed yard and the big black coalmen would come down the side steps and crash the coal into the coal-house until the full number of bags had allegedly been delivered. Then one of us would be asked to count the bags to make sure that the number was correct. It was a ghastly task to have to stand there quaking while the coalman, with only the whites of the eyes showing, lifted one corner of each bag and glared at us. I know that if there had been a bag short I could never have taken on the coalman about it or reported it to my mother. We begged to be let off this job but each time a coal delivery arrived some luckless creature among us was sent down to do the mortifying tally.

CHILDREN HAVE SOME private dreads and one of mine was being told that I looked like my father. It was impossible for a small, fair, skinny girl child to see any resemblance between herself and a tall, brown-haired man who wore spectacles. Not that my father was an unattractive man, but to my way of thinking it killed me off as a person in my own right. I remember gazing at myself in the bathroom mirror when there was a party going on downstairs and I had been told yet again by one of my parents' friends that I was the walking image of my father, and wishing that the bathroom floor would open up and swallow me. He had said that if I were to put on a pair of my father's trousers you couldn't tell us apart, and I really thought I would curl up and die. I used to check whether this man would be among the guests at subsequent parties and time my entries and exits accordingly.

A further example of mind-bending embarrassment was the time I went to a fancy-dress party at school as the 'Producer-Consumer Market'. My mother had asked my father to suggest a costume for me and I hoped it wouldn't be anything too original. My friends were going as Red Ridinghood, the Sugar Plum Fairy, a sailor, a crinolined lady and other recognisable and safe characters. I saw a gleam in my father's eye as he pulled on his pipe and thought about it, and my heart began to sink. 'She could go as the Producer-Consumer

113

Market,' he said with a lift of excitement in his voice, for this had been the topic at government level and he had cartooned it in *Dublin Opinion*. To my horror, a costume was devised despite my pleadings for something ordinary. I was dressed as 'The Producer', a farmer, from the waist up, with a man's shirt and waistcoat, an old felt hat and a basket of carrots and potatoes on my arm. From the waist down I was 'The Consumer', the housewife, and I had to wear a skirt of my mother's and a pair of high-heeled shoes. They said I was sure to win a prize and I got more and more uncomfortable as we went to the event.

When I arrived, my worst fears were realised as my friends, dressed in crinolines and fairy wings, stared at me in amazement which soon turned to amused condescension. Again I thought longingly of person-swallowing floors. I tottered around the hall in the parade and, humiliation of humiliations, I did indeed win a prize for the 'most original costume', to the annoyance of the Sugar Plum Fairy who kicked my shin as I came down from the rostrum in my full agony of exposure.

YOUNG PEOPLE BEGAN to come to Ireland on an exchange basis a year or so after the war. Our first French boy was called Gérard and, having no experience of young continentals, we were thrilled to have him. He had a crew cut, which we thought was rather daring. It was the first time that we had an opportunity of seeing our own country through an outsider's eyes. Wherever he went, people asked him whether he liked Ireland, potatoes and brown bread, and whether life here was much different from life in Paris, until he nearly collapsed from being asked the same questions over and over again. On arrival his lunch box contained a small ceramic pot of pâté and a few hunks of stale bread and we thought this very strange food for a strong lad, compared with our idea of a picnic lunch with plenty of ham, corned beef and other robust fare.

The following year we had a French girl who ate practically nothing on arrival but cleared the boards at every meal by the time she was ready to go home. Although she was only a teenager she wore beautifully cut court shoes and sophisticated suits and she was our first glimpse of La Parisienne. The Abbey Theatre burned down on the night we were to bring her there and transferred to the Queen's some weeks later, where we all enjoyed one of the recurring O'Casey plays, since at that time summer theatre did not offer a very varied programme.

ALMOST ALL OUR CLOTHES were made by dressmakers, sometimes with varying degrees of success. Summer wear for the girls constituted three or four dresses of rather limp cotton, teamed with a school blazer and Clarke's toeless sandals. Special clothes were a wool or velvet dress for important occasions and we were very proud of our 'riding jackets' made for us by a tailor, Mr Jacob, in Dawson Street, to go with our check pleated skirts.

Raincoats were bought every couple of years and were handed down from member to member within our family. They often smelled rather dreadful when they were wet and they were so long that the rain dripped down on the backs of our legs. Rain hats were mainly of the sou'wester type and usually distinctly ugly. I disliked rainwear so much that I hardly ever wore it and preferred to go around damp and steaming rather than get involved with it.

Boys wore rough tweed suits with knee-length trousers, which chapped the backs of their knees in cold weather. They also wore heavy, grey, hand-knitted socks and black leather shoes, the toes of which tended to turn up. A small peaked cap, usually rather dirty from being grabbed off and kicked around the playground, was the finishing touch to their wear.

We loved hair ribbons and constantly washed and ironed ours. When plastic came, we had belts and hairslides made of it, and a big treat was plastic thread in various colours for weaving accessories. Plastic was to change the fabric of many items and was another benchmark in living.

11

Maids

WHEN WE WERE GROWING UP, nearly everyone we knew had a maid, even if there wasn't bread on the table. Most people had a 'living-in' maid and 'Dailies' were a feature in most households. Dailies came in about ten in the morning and remained until about six or so, before leaving for their own homes to do the same kind of work all over again.

The maid was expected to do a little of everything, depending on her talents and inclinations. She didn't have any job definition and it was up to herself to build up the job according to the type of household she had joined. New maids were referred to as 'gems' or 'jewels' for the first few weeks, after which they either turned into a 'disappointment' and had to go, or settled down so well that there was nothing further to say about them.

Some maids liked to cook and immediately took over the kitchen. Others were demon washers, and so the mistress of the house would play the game according to the talents on offer, letting the new maid find her level and, if she were wise, pulling back to suit it. Some were good with children, which meant that the lady of the household could slip into town to meet her friends in Bewley's or Fuller's. Others didn't like children at all and teased them when there was nobody around. Maids got Thursday afternoon and every second Sunday afternoon and evening off. Nobody thought they were hard done by, least of all the girls themselves. They led a somewhat strange life, in but not of the household, with a modicum of authority and as much or as little power as they wished to acquire. As they stayed indoors most of the time, only venturing out to hang clothes on the line or chat to the baker while choosing bread, most of them had pasty faces and were inclined to be on the heavy side.

Friends of ours had a maid called Nonie who ruled them with a fist of iron for ten years. Another family had a maid called Bridie who took over the rearing of the children during the prolonged illness of their mother. Bridie held them all in her power until they were nearly adults and they only escaped her clutches through the happy event of her sudden death. One boy we knew used to give 'Bessie Parties'. He and his friends would gather on the landing outside the maid Bessie's door when she retired early. As she proceeded to groan and snort in her sleep, they would stifle their giggles while they listened to her renderings.

Maids never had anything to do with the 'master' and they preferred it that way. In the majority of households they would bring up the breakfast tray and dump it speechlessly on the master's bed each morning. It therefore came as a vast shock to our Josie when she brought the tray up to my father one morning and, with his eyes still tightly closed, he said, 'Ah go on love, give us a kiss'. He thought it was my mother returning, having left the room while he was asleep. Poor Josie barely managed to get the tray on the bed before fleeing red-faced to the safety of the kitchen. When my father's fury at his mistake had died down, my mother had to sort the whole thing out with the shaken Josie lest she pack her one case and go.

Maids did not seem unhappy, apart from their fits of sulks and 'just being difficult'. Because their position and their duties were not clearly defined, they often had greater liberty than they would have had in their own homes. They ran their lives to their own satisfaction in most cases, usually leaving to marry and settle down, possessed of a good knowledge of running a home and minding children.

OVER THE YEARS we had several girls, starting with various Josies and Mollies and passing then from Mary to Mary. We liked most of them and they would ask us children to read them their letters from home. We revelled in the accounts of life in the country and often we did not quite follow the narrative, as verbs and other key words were lacking or punctuation was sparse. We would omit the summons home if there was one, for the mothers of these girls often called them back once they had received a good training in someone else's home, regretting having given them their independence.

Naturally romance reared its head in the lives of the maids and they would often let us in on the state of their affairs. We had one girl who would leave us each year for her holidays at home, hoping to meet a nice lad and all set for a bit of magic. One of us would trim her hair for her and we would admire her new dresses from the sales before she went off with high hopes, but each year the same thing would happen. A sad work-worn little figure would return, having slaved for the two weeks at home, cleaning up after relatives from England or cooking day and night during harvest time. This girl never seemed to have any luck with the men but eventually she became completely infatuated with John, a man from 'Shicargo'. He used to come over to spend his holidays in his mother's boarding house, and to our Mary this man was all the film stars rolled into one, a cross between Cary Grant and James Stewart with a good dash of Gregory Peck. She should have been over the stage of admiring men from afar and have been into more practical applications, but hers was a hopeless case. We would do her hair for her on her evening off when John was home, and down she would go to the boarding house to gaze at him. This went on for a couple of years until her treasured John arrived home unexpectedly with an American bride. Mary became old in an evening and left us not long

118

afterwards, upset over something trivial.

The next maid but one was also called Mary. She replaced a girl who used to tear pages out of cookery books to light cigarettes from the gas stove, and was, therefore, asked to leave. This Mary was all go. She did vast washings, cooked repasts of many courses, cleaned up after endless sittings of meals and got through mounds of ironing without apparent effort. We thought we were made up for life. Mary's compensation for all this work was to fling herself into bed for an hour or two every afternoon. She would rise refreshed at about four o'clock, put on a clean dress, wash the one she had taken off and hang it out, and then make a cup of tea to bring up to my mother who would also have taken a nap. She actually had only three dresses, all cotton, one on her, one on the clothes-line and one ready to wear. She would round on the house-work once more and tear into the preparation of the evening meal, and when we all came charging in there would be surprises of all sorts cooking up in the depths of the Aga.

Mary's home was a lively place if we were to believe her stories. These stories had a pre-Russian Revolutionary flavour, such as being beaten by her father whenever he took a notion. If her sisters were feeling jealous or wanted to prevent her from going to a dance, they would put her dress in the rain barrel 'as a sort of a joke'. She related how they had a tough time breaking her father off the use of a jug and getting him onto cups in time for her sister's wedding, and how her mother beat them if they came in late. Mary was very vain and spent all her money on shoes, in spite of having unbelievably large feet, and her favourite shoes were a pair of blue suede canal barges with large ribbons flapping at the prow.

When she eventually left, we missed her greatly. No more would we see her vigorous form pulling rhubarb in the back garden while we sat at the dinner table mystified as to her next move, for Mary liked surprises and would come crashing through the door with a steaming rhubarb concoction minutes after she had pulled the raw materials. Her cookery ranged from such instant dishes to slow cooking ones secretly prepared and lovingly brought to completion in the depths of the ovens. The boys missed her when the cat had kittens for Mary always ran a sweep on the number expected and the basement was strangely quiet when she left. She probably went off to marry her intended and make rhubarb tarts for herself.

12

Illness and Death

Illness was quite different from what it is nowadays as many vaccines had not yet been developed. It was still in recent memory that people suffering from pneumonia always came to a crisis, after which they either lived or died. Children had only recently been rescued from death by diphtheria, which was a condition whereby a web grew in the back of the throat, eventually closing it over and suffocating the patient. Ringworm was not unusual and children caught it in their heads, which meant that all their hair had to be shaven off to have treatment. The bonus was that their hair nearly always grew luxuriantly afterwards. Cancer was never mentioned by name. 'The Lad' was the sympathetic form of allusion and it was an illness that was often denied. Tuberculosis was still about and most people knew someone in a sanatorium, so if anyone started to fling open windows out of season it was assumed that there was tuberculosis in that home.

Mental illness was absolutely taboo. The general thinking was that there was hardly any difference between a nervous illness and someone being 'right off their head' or even 'a little strange in themselves', and across the whole spectrum of mental illness a blanket was thrown. Horror stories naturally abounded in this area and as children we enjoyed regaling one another with tales about the padded cells in which we thought mad people bounced themselves around untiringly. I even thought that the cells were upholstered in pink and white striped cotton and that the food for the patient came in liquid form through a tube in the wall, so that the poor unfortunate could apply his or her lips for a snack between bounces. We would exchange knowing glances passing mental institutions or 'lunatic asylums' as they were called.

Of the ordinary childhood diseases scarlet fever was the most serious and a child who contracted it either had to be quarantined at home or go to Temple Street Children's Hospital. When one of us went down with it my mother carried out the quarantine regulations with absolute strictness, as if she did not have enough to do otherwise in running the household. Some years later scarlet fever broke out once more and most of the schools had to be closed. I was taken quite unawares one day when I was having a bath and I fainted down under the bath water. I did not know I had contracted the fever although I was feeling rather odd. The bathroom door was locked, for modesty ran high in those days and purposeful locking of bathroom doors took place before people even washed their faces. I came to with water lapping around my ears, and after many attempts clambered out of the bath and lay on the linoleum floor between faints. Linoleum was top of the list for bathroom coverings at the time. Eventually, freezing and shaking violently, I was able to wrap myself in a towel, unlock the door and cry for help.

Anaesthetics were administered by a horrible means. The doctor put a large rubber bag like a collapsed football over people's faces and a nurse held them down while they wriggled backwards and forwards, trying to escape the gas issuing from it. They did it to me once when I was having a toe lanced as a small child and I nearly lost my reason. For many years afterwards I had a recurring nightmare of being held down to screaming point. I even eyed croquet hoops gingerly, thinking they could be used to pin people down against their will.

We were very fond of tonics in our house. People were constantly building themselves up for greater things and the variety of tonics was large. As small children we had been lined up every morning for cod liver oil and Parish's food mixture, a concoction prepared by the chemist and delivered in a huge family-sized bottle. It was red in colour when the oil separated and went to the top, and it was regarded by most families as a passport to health. Then came 'Roboline', a soft, toffee-like substance which we liked so much that we ate it straight out of the jar and thoroughly sickened ourselves. Calcium tablets were handed out daily from a green tin box and were as much a part of the morning routine as breakfast. I took all cures and preventive measures seriously and would obligingly have swallowed golf balls if I thought they were good for me.

BEAUTY CARE WAS also popular, and when we were small we girls used to put Vaseline on our eyelashes before going to sleep. I used the Vaseline from my bicycle puncture repair kit and never missed a night when I put it on, returning it to the saddle bag the next day. We went through a phase of having a teaspoonful of olive oil daily to make our nails strong and we always put a drop of vinegar or lemon juice in the rinsing water when we washed our hair. We joyously embraced the Pond's Cold Cream Seven Day Beauty Plan at an early age and used to examine ourselves minutely for improvement on the seventh day each time we performed the ritual. We were expected to look smart most of the time and spot-checks on nails were quite frequent. Warts were regarded with horror and we put Union Jack paste on them if they appeared, burning the skin and the offending wart. We also tried to banish them by anointing them with saliva while still fasting each morning, a process which we firmly believed would remove them.

SOMETHING WHICH INTERESTED me very much was the daily report on infectious diseases published in the press. These records were registered at the Dublin city dispensaries, and erysipelas, diphtheria, measles, chicken pox and scarlet fever were among the maladies charted. I used to get the paper each day and inspect their progress, disappointed when the figures dropped and delighted when they rose, rather like following investments on the stock exchange.

Death was something which we did not have to come to terms with for many years. Our grandparents had died early, and out of four of them I could only remember one grandfather dozing by the fire in my aunt's house, while I assessed the drawer in the table for pencils. I had had one eye on him and one eye on the pencils and the pencils were more important to me. Like most children we were extremely interested in funerals and not at all afraid of them. We watched them with the greatest of interest and stood on our toes to see if anyone in the funeral cars was crying. Death was something which happened to other people and not to us, rather like other people's houses burning down. We even took to burying toys with full ceremony, my doll, Esmeralda, spending a few nights under the clay wrapped in an old tablecloth. Likewise we buried worms in matchboxes and put up little crosses over them.

The first person I remember dying was a man in Blackrock who was not the full shilling and who used to run after me holding my carrier when I was on my little blue bicycle. I was mortally afraid of Jack, whom everyone else regarded as harmless, which he probably was. When he died suddenly I was absolutely thrilled as I had not thought there was any way out of my horror of being chased by him, 'a poor lad who meant no harm'. Death therefore was not classified by me as a disaster as I had thought that I was going to have Jack for life. It was only when my best friend told me that her sister was dying that the matter came into perspective.

This sister was our great ally, our source of fountain pens, the odd bit of cash and our best audience for self-styled forms of entertainment. Although I had known that she was ill I had not been told that it was so serious. The two of us were walking back from the hockey field on a dark winter's afternoon locked in conversation when my friend confided that her sister was dying. I began to giggle, taken aback by my friend's solemn little face, and then we both collapsed with laughter. We stood there in the gathering dark and laughed ourselves inside out, then sank on the damp grass and laughed ourselves out completely. Finally we faced each other shamefacedly and got up slowly, looking around for the hockey sticks thrown down in the first great burst of mirth. We walked back together in silence, very embarrassed and confused, for death had touched us for the first time and it could never be funny again, now that it had to do with someone we knew and loved. The sister recovered but we never mentioned the episode to one another and death did not concern us again for many years.

In any case, we didn't feel threatened by it as we were safe in the knowledge that Catholics nearly always went to Heaven. Even those caught in Purgatory en route eventually arrived safely, usually helped by the prayers and penances carried out on their behalf, so it was not really a situation to spend time thinking about.

13

Christmas

CHRISTMAS WAS a marathon every year. Turkeys were bought and delivered without being cleaned out, and only the very fussy would have paid a butcher to do the job for them. It was considered rather unsporting not to clean out your own turkey and there was always the widespread belief that if you left yours in the butcher's to have the job done for you, turkeys might be switched and you might not get the one you paid for. Pulling the sinews of the turkey was part of the preparation and this involved great sweating and straining on the part of fathers who always got the job. They had first to locate the said sinews and then pull them with an array of tools from the toolbox. It was a complex job but it was taken for granted that if there was a man in the house at all, the very least he might do was to draw the sinews of the turkey.

The cleaning out was a gruesome business and mothers did this valiantly. First of all the kitchen table was thickly spread with newspapers and then the slow, careful evisceration began. Most of us avoided the kitchen during the operation, but those who entered in had to be stout of heart as it was unwise to stand there and wrinkle your nose at the proceedings if you intended to enjoy your turkey in a day or two – and my mother would tell you so. It was also taken for granted that cooking the Christmas dinner was a complicated business and involved using every piece of cutlery in the house. The amount of testing, poking, lifting, stirring and shaking that went on required the use of many utensils and receptacles, as without refrigeration it was not customary to prepare food in advance, and everything tended to come to a climax on the cooker at the same time.

Sometimes part of the laundry got in the way of the cooking as life had to go on, willy-nilly, with nine people in the house and no washing machine. Clean handkerchiefs were much in demand in cold weather and these always boiled in a huge pot during Christmas as at any other time. The maid was often in the sulks at such an invasion of the kitchen and might retire to her room for a while to mark her displeasure. It was normal that maids did not go home for Christmas and they were expected to get over it quickly. And so, cooking, washing, discussion, laughter, washing up, gossiping, testing with groans of appreciation and chatter all went on at the same time, with a through-passage of children all excited about Christmas. The pudding boiled and hissed and had to be given many hours of boiling. Brandy butter was beaten with wooden bats, and a succession of sauces was organised, apple, bread and cranberry being some of them.

Christmas dinner was built around the turkey and ham. To us children the turkey was by far the more interesting of the two but as usual there was always an endless fuss about the ham. Conversation leading up to Christmas would deal with the ham rather than anything else and enormous care went into its cooking. In the morning it would be boiled and then simmered for a number of hours, tested, put back for further simmering, tested again and pronounced delicious. Then it would be put to one side to give attention to everything else. I always thought it tasted rather ordinary, having eaten ham every weekend, week in, week out, in some form or other, but I can still hear my mother's phrase at the first bite of Christmas ham each year: 'The ham is a poem....'

The turkey was always a dream, a large free-range hen turkey, crunchy and delicious with exquisite, juicy, herby stuffing escaping from its neck to roast into a further crust. I dearly loved the turkey's liver roasted separately and my mother used to slip this to me in the general confusion. It was the only piece of cooking done specially for me that I can remember and this annual turkey liver eaten discreetly was to me what the annual bottle of very special and expensive wine is to some people, something to be savoured as the crystallisation of a very important occasion.

The vast array of vegetables all coming to the table at the same time was as puzzling to children as the ham business. How sprouts, celery, carrots, parsnips and other vegetables could suddenly assume great importance was a mystery, when there were also crispy roast potatoes, dishes of creamed potatoes and so many sauces to be investigated.

The pudding was further cause for excitement. We always forgot to turn off the light before setting it aflame and someone would have to fling themselves at the switch to darken the room so that we could admire the blue flames dancing around the top of it before charring of the surface set in. Eating Christmas pudding on top of such a vast dinner was never regarded as overdoing things and everyone downed large platefuls smothered in brandy butter and sometimes brandy cream as well. There was always a giant fruit salad standing by in case anyone was still feeling peckish.

HEATING THE HOUSE was a priority at Christmas time and there would be fires blazing in many of the rooms. The kitchen would be going full blast with the Aga cooker and the Aga water heater, and there would be heaters on landings, with draughts heated en route to wherever draughts go.

To our minds one of the particularly enjoyable parts of Christmas dinner was getting our Aunt Aggie tipsy. She had vowed total abstinence which made her a real challenge to the lower element in the company. We would make sure that she was seated with her back to a painting and when she was well into her second glass of lemonade we would ask her to turn around and admire the 'new' picture. We would then add a lightning tot of whiskey to her glass, previously siphoned off from the bottle for the purpose and sit back for the pleasure of her company. Aggie would be ours as we plied her with questions and she gave us answers as to how many men there had been in her life and how many she had left broken-hearted. She would be quite flushed at her sudden popularity and eventually the respectable people at the top of the table would become jealous at the waves of laughter coming from our end and ask to be let in on the jokes. This we could not do for we needed Aggie for the following year.

CHRISTMAS PRESENTS were kept heavily secret. One year I hid mine so well that I did not find them till the following March and I had to be helped to finance a second round. Another year, one brother bought some books of raffle tickets as a shrewd move and decided that these would surely cover his Christmas presents to the family. The prizes offered were many and generous and according to his reckoning the odds were in his favour. The hamper would go to mother, the bottles of wine to father and the family would get the runner-up prizes. He bought one ticket in the name of each person and one or two over to cover the odds. He then went off and spent all his Christmas money on Meccano building systems. The results would be published in the *Irish Press* on 21 December. On that date he went down to Blackrock and bought a paper, but to his horror he could not find any of our names among the prizewinners in the Great Christmas Draw. He too received financial assistance on a strictly confidential basis.

Another brother could never get his Christmas cards done in time for posting and anyway he didn't know the addresses of any of his friends. Each year he had to be taken out in the car on Christmas Eve on a private run, red-eyed and in despair, to push unstamped Christmas cards through the letter boxes of the houses in which he thought his friends lived. Every Christmas he requested a *Curly Wee Book* and would sit on the floor with his back to the chesterfield and read it aloud from one end to the other, whether anyone was listening or not. It was his personal Christmas treat and he loved it.

THE CHRISTMAS PANTOMIME was a must every year and Jimmy O'Dea reigned supreme and was joined by the inimitable Maureen Potter. As a child I either immediately liked or actively disliked entertainment and I never liked pantomime as I was mortally afraid of the principal boy because I could not understand what he/she signified. Being a logical child and confronted by a female person dressed in high boots and tights before ever they became high fashion, I couldn't figure it out. I also felt injured because every time the story got going someone would hold up things by bursting into song. I would be at the point of tears with frustration but I would never have dreamed of dropping out of going to the pantomime as a Christmas outing.

IT WAS THE TIME when people first started having their Christmas cards printed. Formal greetings were to become 'dernier cri' and otherwise perfectly normal people who had always penned 'love from Paddy, Ros and the gang' were now sending cards with 'Patrick and Rose O'Rourke send you a warm seasonal wish' printed on them in heavy type. Their friends and relations were slamming back with 'Kind thoughts from Robert and Margaret McGrath' when it had always been 'Cheers from Bob, Peg and Co'. Even close relatives served each other with these missives for some years before the craze died out with an unexpected increase in printing and posting charges.

SANTY WAS A LADY one year, to the shock of juvenile Dún Laoghaire. The Santy in Woolworth's was the most active in the district and the most on display since we bought many of our Christmas presents there. To our horror one year Santy came out of his booth and turned around to get something. This action revealed a split in his gown, a large backside and a pair of silk-clad stout legs and high-heeled shoes. The shock was compounded for our family members as on closer inspection we recognised a cleaning lady from our area, who was rosy-complexioned and plump, and was presumably doing a nixer for the Christmas season.

Santies differed from shop to shop, and in McKinley's Santy was the messenger boy dressed in a red dressing-gown and wellingtons, pink of face and frightened of eye behind a large uneven beard. As business was somewhat slack the manager was heard to order him off to sweep out the back of the shop and it was a poor sight indeed to see Santy so suddenly demoted.

BAREFOOT CHILDREN WERE a normal sight in Dublin and when we went into town at Christmas time we saw plenty of them in O'Connell Street with the small pinched faces of the poor. These children had shaved heads and were often black with dirt and were unhappily part of the normal Dublin street scene.

The excitement of our Christmas visit to town was heightened by the journey home by train. We would meet my father at the station and leave from Tara Street, all bunched together clutching presents from Santy, of no particular value or endurance. Sparks would fly and then suddenly the big sooty engine would whirl towards us. We would fling ourselves at the door of the carriage, pressing to get in before the train raced away again without us. It was usually full of men with bulky Crombie coats who lit up pipes to their satisfaction while settling back to discuss their jobs in government departments or the Corporation and although they were comparatively young they were settled in their way, encased in a safe world of jobs and families. Women civil servants and office girls would fumble in large bags and bring out inexplicable knitting in indiscriminate colours to finish off someone's Christmas present.

We would chew silently on toffee bars, while we absorbed the warmth and movement of the train and checked the brightly-lit windows at the back of the houses, where women were busily getting the evening meal. Blackrock station always came as a shock, cold, black and wet with the east wind howling over the sea wall. We would rush over the naked windswept footbridge and up Bath Avenue into Blackrock, longing to be safely home, and then hurry up George's Avenue, the wind-tunnel that led there. And so Christmas came and went each year, a mixture of mystery, excitement and banality and we could never have imagined it being celebrated any other way.

14

The Country

FOR MANY YEARS we went to the country on holidays for most of July. We stayed in a large farm guesthouse in Ballinglen, County Wicklow, between Aughrim and Tinahely and for suburban children the interlude was a dream come true. The sounds of the farm were very important to us and as we prepared for the holiday we would imitate the noises from memory to heighten our anticipation. They were the noise of the rasping porch door of the old Georgian farmhouse, the wide galvanised iron gate into the farmyard which bonged to a close when the farm-hands had seen the last of the milking herd through each evening, the smart click of the red door in the yard wall when you lifted its latch and the 'lub-dub', 'lub-dub' of the ram which pumped water into the house around the clock.

We were off to a world of soft leafy lanes and sun-flecked hedgerows, the harsh croak of the corncrake, the larks suspended against the sun over huge smooth fields of grazing herds, the steady brown river where we unsuccessfully tried to fish each year and the sparkling streams which we would spend hours damming, the feel of the early morning air on our young skins and the animal smells of the farmyard. There would be rides on the tractor with Johnny Fox and high jumps to be taken into the bales of last year's hay in the barns.

The farms in west Wicklow were mainly large holdings with family members working adjoining properties. Fertilisers had not yet been developed; the fields were strewn with wild flowers and there were so many varieties of these that we would stand in one spot and see how many we could gather. The cowslips had a slightly hypnotic odour and we would bury our noses in them feeling a little high and wondering why. The hedgerows were laced with honeysuckle and haw-thorn and underneath the soft damp leaves in the banks of the lanes there were wild strawberries and raspberries. Sometimes we were there for the onset of the mushrooms and we would go out early for the excitement of finding the clumps of but-tons. Crab apples grew on the gnarled old trees down in the bog and we ate these on principle although they were so sour that they cut our gums, as we felt honour-bound to explore this world so far from our life in Blackrock.

BALLINGLEN WAS a large residence with sets of staircases leading to different parts of the house. Under one of them there was a children's library made up of all the reading of the Boyd family down through the years, and this meant for us the luxury of a whole new set of adventure books. There was a music-box in the drawing-room which played 'Charlie is my Darling' type songs and we used to curl up in the old soft sofas on wet days and listen to it. Each year we travelled by train as there was a petrol shortage, and coming down the branch line from Rathdrum the twigs brushed the carriage windows on each side until we reached Ballinglen station, which was like something out of a child's storybook. The first thing we did on arrival at the farm was to select a stick suit-able for poking things. Either we cut one specially or combed the haggard and fields and found one abandoned by someone else. Thus armed, we would set about enjoying our holiday in earnest.

There were excursions as well as on-the-spot entertainment. One was a trip to the forge where there was a chance of seeing the smith's right hand. The skin of his palm had grown over so thickly down the years that he could only open it about an inch and we looked forward to viewing this horrifying sight, the very blackness of the skin adding to the macabre effect. There was also the early morning journey to the creamery. We would get up about six or so, pull on summer dresses, cardigans and sandals and steal furtively out of the house, creak down the wide and shallow staircase and out into the dewy morning, run down the tree-lined avenue and wait by the road for the cart to come rattling by. Then we would leap out and beg the men to bring us with them. They would yank us up on the cart and we would all rattle away, holding on to the churns to stop falling off, and shouting to one another above the noise. There would be a wait at the creamery while we nearly starved to death for want of a breakfast and then we would be bounced back on the cart as the empty churns did not offer much in the way of support.

Sheep-dipping, hand-milking, calf-rearing and manifold activities of the farm took up our time and we barely managed to attend for meals, driven in by hunger. We wore wellingtons practically the whole time although they rubbed our heels, as they were a fail-safe precaution against something really interesting happening on the farm from which wearing sandals would have excluded us. The holiday photographs always showed us wearing summer dresses with uneven hems from being caught in hedges, wellingtons and hand-knitted cardigans. The Boyd family were most understanding about our enthusiasm, although we often did things out of innocence which astonished them. We washed kittens, brought in clutches of eggs that were about to hatch in the belief that they were newly laid and fed the hens sawdust for the excitement of seeing them gather for an unexpected snack.

My father would spend much of the holiday painting water colours of the countryside and my mother would read out of doors, sitting on a log or in the porch if the wind was too fresh. We would go for walks with her in the evenings, along mysterious lanes, and she always had a supply of sweets which she produced unexpectedly when the walk was well under way. Then we would all swing along with a bulls-eye in one cheek, poking things with our sticks and having great conversations. We enjoyed these walks so much that we would beg for them even if the weather was poor, setting out in fair weather and returning soaking wet. The only shop in the district was at Walsh's post office, but we didn't get pocket money in the country. The system was that large drums of Lemon's pure sweets were packed for the holiday and these were doled out in daily rations, so that you could either eat them all at once or spread them over the day, depending on your disposition.

THE BOYDS HAD an Aunt Maggie who lived with them and we knew her as Miss Hadden. She put great store on age, asking us children what age we were and crying, 'Well done, well done!' when we informed her. We would feel full of self-confidence as a result of this attention. She was an elegant old lady always dressed in black and wore good jewellery, and she spent her days sitting in the sunny porch in a basket chair which she had bought on a cruise to Madeira, knitting little squares to be sewn into a blanket. She conducted games of 'Twenty Questions' in which anyone could join, and she was highly popular. Occasionally she took a day in bed and she would invite us in to her room. One of us would engage her in conversation while another peered carefully at all her memorabilia. On her good days she would set off to the post office using a blackthorn stick for support. She also used it to beat down fifty thistles on the way there and fifty thistles on the way back, doing her bit for the environment.

One day I met her coming back at a gentle pace, as she was about ninety at the time. I fell into step with her, but I soon got bored with the slow pace and regretted my burst of companionship; not wishing to be impolite I decided to do something about it. When we came to a stile in the high bank along the road I suggested going over it for a short cut. Miss Hadden was entranced at the suggestion as she hadn't done anything so daring for decades, and I proceeded to show her where to hook in her stick, quite oblivious of the danger to which I was exposing her. I then put my shoulder under her rear and hooshed her up from one level to the next until at last I got her up on the bank in standing position, where she remained for some time flushed in triumph and surveying the view. I was delighted not to have to drag down the avenue with her and felt completely in control as I lowered her down from flag to flag on the other side. We then took a short cut across the lawn to the house where I was taken aback to see people running towards us who had spotted us out of a top window. Miss Hadden was gleaming with victory but I was taken aside and admonished severely about possible broken hips.

I was greatly smitten by one of the older sons on the farm. He was tall with unblinking brown eyes and had the allure of being an inaccessible Protestant. He sometimes gave us rides on Cash the pony and when it came to my turn to be lifted up or down I would go limp so that I could slither down him and marginally extend the only physical contact I was ever likely to have with him. He played cricket well at the matches arranged in the barn every evening, and I would sit on a bale of hay and admire him, longing to be hit by a cricket ball, with visions of myself lying under the washed-out cotton bedspread with a cracked head while he came to enquire about my injuries.

OVER THE YEARS we got to know the local people. This little-visited part of Wicklow had its own forms of speech and a feature of the language were the slightly off-target words. A 'vacancy' behind the chimney was a cavity, a 'scrap goat' was the victim of persecution, the 'sanctuaristy' was the place to which you went to have a Mass said, and following a hard winter people said that they had all been 'in the one leprosy'. Children were called 'chaps', irrespective of gender and nice-looking girls were called 'prutty'. A hot 'fornication' went on a boil and neighbours sometimes died of 'hardening of the archeries'.

This was a slumbering corner of Wicklow with narrow roads leading to Moyne, Askinagap and Ballymanus, with high hedges and pony and trap transport clopping along without fear of motor traffic. Solitary people wobbled by on bicycles and in one of the villages there lived a family known locally as 'The Informers'. The informing had been done over a century and a half earlier during the 1798 insurrection, but the children in the family descended from the legendary informer still hung their heads and had nothing to do with the other children in the district.

ONE AFTERNOON on the farm a most thrilling event was to take place. We got wind of it when we were told in the morning that the yard would be out of bounds for the whole afternoon, and we hung around earwigging as to why. It was the day on which mares belonging to neighbours were to be brought to be covered by Dano the stallion, who was normally kept locked up in his stable with his head sticking out through a slit in the wall. We heard the farm-hands discussing the form and resolved to witness what would surely be something very exciting. After an early lunch we slipped in by the haggard and cow sheds and flashed up the outside staircase to the corn loft to set ourselves up in style for the spectacle. We placed boxes in a row a good bit back from the window and got handfuls of corn ready to eat as if we were going to the pictures and had boxes of Smarties. For suburban children this was going to be something out of the ordinary.

The men emerged from the farm kitchen and took off their jackets. Dano's stable door was opened and he clattered out with three men handling him. The first mare was brought across the yard showing the whites of her eyes, and our excitement reached fever pitch so that we forgot and moved ever closer to the window. Just at the point of encounter, Mr Boyd caught a glimpse of a red jersey and he stopped the whole theatre. We heard heavy steps mounting the staircase, the door was flung open and there was a shout of 'Out chaps! All out and fast!' Crestfallen and thoroughly mortified, we crept down the steps with the farm-hands laughing at us, dropping corn as we went and bitterly disappointed at the collapse of our afternoon's entertainment.

FOSSETS' CIRCUS wintered their animals in the stables behind the old mill at Ballinglen bridge. Sometimes we went for walks there in the evenings and one evening my father slipped into an empty shed and let the party go ahead. He then gave a lion's roar which sent people fleeing in all directions. Walks were full of surprises.

Every summer the tinkers came to camp below the bridge, and worked in tin, rerimming wheels and repairing worn farm implements and household utensils. They beat out sheets of metal to make casings, mended sieves and put handles on pots, bringing up to date all the items collected over the year for repair. At that time the tinkers liked their name for they worked in tin and they took their place in the local economy as much as the blacksmith did and were respected accordingly. They were all known by name by the local farmers and sometimes had meals in their kitchens. When plastic arrived and pushed aside the use of tin to a large extent, the tinkers lost their trade and their standing and the main source of their income. 'Tinker' became a pejorative word, and eventually the tinkers came no more to Ballinglen bridge.

THE EVENINGS IN Ballinglen were lovely when the birds and animals were settling down after the day. The sun would slant across the gently-rounded hills and the pine forests would provide dark bands of contrast with the soft greenery. Velvety shadows would steal across the meadows and we thought there was nowhere in the world as lovely as Ballinglen. We loved it so much that one day when my mother spotted an advertisement for a forester's cottage at nearby Aughrim which was to be sold by tender, she persuaded my father to put in a bid. They decided to go to three hundred pounds for it as it was on the edge of a plantation and overlooked the valley towards Rathdrum. When my father was leaving for town the day he was going to put in the tender, my mother ran after him and said, 'Make it three hundred and ten'. He did and we got the cottage, just pipping Dr Noel Browne to the post.

Now we were landowners, with a pine-clad hillside to call our own if we wanted to and a valley lying smiling before us. We had outgrown the farm holidays and the cottage was to be a source of continual enjoyment, offering the exquisite certainty that there was always somewhere to go. Although it was only 50 miles form home it was in a different world and the novelty of it never wore off. It was faithfully minded for us for nearly forty years by Patsy and Nan Kennedy of Rednagh.

OUR FRIENDS TOOK holiday homes up the coast in places like Bettystown and Rush in the area known as 'the northern beaches'. In inadequate kitchens made of chipboard, they cooked up monster meals on ancient cookers for one of the summer months, and catered for hoards of sandy, happy children called in from the vast clean beaches and dunes. We had friends in Rush who had bought three single-decker buses and joined them up into a zig-zag, and we loved the Sunday outings when they invited us all down for the day to sample their kind of holiday.

THEN CAME THE INITIAL gentle rending of the fabric of our childhood when the first visible sputnik successfully circled the earth at the end of the 1950s. We had followed its progress with enormous interest, and now this eighth wonder of the world was scheduled to pass at about five o'clock in the morning over eastern Ireland, which to us meant Blackrock. We all got up shortly after four and met in the hall for the drive down to Idrone Terrace on the seafront, for a good view. A number of people had come down to see the sputnik and we all waited in the morning chill with that spirit of camaraderie which springs up around strangers who have come together at an odd time for a purpose well beyond the normal course of life. Then we saw it.

The Soviets had kept their promise and the blue-black sky was pierced by an extra star which emerged slowly and then

became sharper in outline until it sparkled across the heavens, faded and disappeared. It left us behind in every sense and I was suddenly aware that change had found a way into our own safe world. The thread of permanence which had ruled it for so long had stretched and snapped and things could never be the same again.